Forward

Since 1966, I have been a professional boxing promoter, matchmaker, manager, and consultant. Some of the boxer's I have worked with include **Sonny Liston, George Foreman, Muhammed Ali**, Cedric Boswell, Robert Allen, Ismael Laguna, Oscar Bonavena, Ken Buchanan, Johnny Gant, Ken Norton, Iran Barkley, Emile Griffith, and many others. If you are not a well-trained fighter, you need to know how to protect yourself. As Mr. Gordon accurately notes, todays Covid-19, unemployment, social unrest, and growing poverty have created a different world than we lived in only five years ago. Merely taking a leisurely walk outside or to your car puts you at risk.

A solid hickory one-diameter solid hickory cane is a great equalizer. Black-belt masters have been clocked with radar guns swinging a cane at 200+ mph. That said, you should be able to swing your cane at half that speed or better. What effective protection!!! While it is illegal to walk around with a baseball bat, for health reasons you can carry a unique walking cane even if it is solid hickory wood.

Most important, as Mr. Gordon emphasizes, three-quarters of dangerous situations can be avoided with common sense and cane spinning. Don't be unprotected in today's world when it so easy to carry a walking cane.

Harry Barnett

Four Types of People Who Need This Book

Young and Healthy

You don't need a cane to walk, but you are vulnerable to attacks and need a system of self-defense. With your speed and endurance, you become a formidable opponent from an attack.

Elderly but Vigorous

Although you do not need a cane to walk, you appear vulnerable on the street and could therefore become a target. A cane could be your best bet for self-defense.

Cane Dependent

You need a cane to walk safely. If attacked, you could lean against a building for support or sit on the ground or a bench, then use the cane with two hands to defend yourself.

Wheelchair Bound

You use a wheelchair because you are elderly, paraplegic (perhaps a wounded soldier), or recovering from an injury. You could use a cane to defend yourself quite effectively from a seated position.

Time is the coin of your life…Be careful least you let other people spend it for you. Carl Sandburg

Or, worse, take it from you. It is your job to protect the only life you have. Ted Gordon

Other Books by Ted H. Gordon

Law Books
California Real Estate Law: Text and Cases

Legal Terminology and Usage: For Court Reporters and Paralegals

Individuals with Disabilities Education Act: Handbook for Special Education Teachers and Parents

Medical Books
Live, Don't Let Cancer Become Your Life: Handle Your Disease, and Make Good Medical Decisions

Burdens of the Heart: Surviving Heart Transplant and Finding Secrets of the Medical Profession

C. diff: What is it? How do you get this disease? How do you get rid of it?

Martial Arts Books
Escape Being Raped or Attacked: Using Common Sense, Karate, and Ju-Jitsu

Defend Yourself with Ju-Jitsu and Karate and Stay Out of Jail

Business Books
Summary of Parliamentary Procedure

Real Estate Principles in California (Co-Author)

Children's Book
How a Poor Student Became the World's Smartest Man: The Story of Albert Einstein

Cane Jitsu Defense

Second Edition

Ted H. Gordon, MBA, JD
Third-Degree Black Belt, Ju-Jitsu
Brown Belt, Karate

Marinwood Publisher

© 2021 by Ted H. Gordon

All rights reserved. No parts of this book may be reproduced or used in any form or by any means graphic, mechanical, digital, or audio (including but not limited to photocopying, recording, taping, Web distribution, information storage, and digital retrieval system) without the prior express written permission of the author.

However, any person may copy up to one paragraph as fair use provided (1) no words are changed, (2) full attribution is given, and (3) the use is part of another book, a review, or an analysis.

Printing: (July 2021)

Second Edition

ISBN-13:   **978-1-7374659-0-4**
Printed in the United States

 Marinwood Publishers

Table of Contents

1. Introduction to the Cane 1
2. Situational Awareness 21
3. Strikes 29
4. Blocks 47
5. Stances and Positions 57
6. Figure-8, The Best Move in this Book 67
7. Pressure Points 77
8. Nature of Punching Attacks 89
9. Defense to Punches 99
10. Defense to Kicks 113
11. Defense Against Holds 121
    A. Front Choke 122
    B. Rear Bear Hug 125
    C. Front Bear Hug 127
    D. Rear Hand Choke 129
    E. Lapel Grip 132
    F. Wrist Grips 133
12. Cane Grabs 137
13. Cane Spinning 149
14. Defending Multiple Attackers 163
15. Wheelchair Defense 173
16. Elderly Seniors Defense 199
    • Appendix (Where to Buy Self-Defense Canes) 213

Dedicated to

Mark Shuey, Sr. and Joe Robaina, the two Grandmasters in modern America who are most responsible for popularizing the use and acceptance of the cane for self-defense

Disclaimer, Waiver, and Release

Being attacked is a dangerous situation, and no book, including this one, can promise you that its self-defense techniques will protect you, prevent you from injuries, or even be effective in an attack. Your attacker may have special skills you did not realize; the aggressor may luckily move in a way to block a technique; you may be so frozen with fear that you will forget the technique, or do it wrong; you could be so hyped up with adrenaline that you do the move incorrectly or ineffectively; or a hundred other things could render the techniques ineffective.

To the full extent permitted by law, the author makes no warranties, express or implied (including but not limited to implied warranties of merchantability and fitness for a particular purpose). Use the techniques and information in this book at your own risk. THIS BOOK IS PRESENTED SOLELY FOR ACADEMIC STUDY.

The author is not liable for any damages, incurred or alleged to have incurred, of any kind arising from the use or non-use of the information or techniques in this book, including but not limited to direct, indirect, incidental, punitive, or consequential damages. You further agree not to sue the author and to hold him harmless from any all claims arising out of the information and techniques contained in this book.

If you disagree with any of the above, return this book within 30 days after purchase for a refund, and do not use any of the information and techniques contained in it.

How to Practice

<u>Be Kind to Yourself</u>. Imagine you were standing in a cane defense class and your neighbor complained of being frustrated. You would most likely turn and remind him or her that this is a sport like golf or tennis. You would remind your neighbor that you do not learn a sport in an hour. It takes time and many repetitions. Be as kind to yourself as you would be to a stranger next to you. Give yourself time to learn and do not expect to pick up everything on the first attempt.

<u>Dangerous—Practice with Instructor.</u> The techniques discussed in this book can be dangerous, causing severe injury, and possibly even death. They can be hazardous to practice and are even more deadly if done wrong. Make the moves with the help of a qualified instructor who can control the speed and method of performing the techniques and correct improper technique.

<u>Doctors Approval</u>. Practicing the techniques in the book is a form of exercise, and one should never engage in physical activity without a doctor's approval.

<u>Look Out for Your Partner</u>. If you choose to practice without a qualified instructor—never a good idea—remember that neither you nor your practicing partner is likely skilled in the martial arts. Take special precautions to protect your partner. Never hit your partner; always stop your attacks and strikes several inches from your opponent. Stop immediately if your partner yells "stop" or otherwise suggests submission.

Layman's Knowledge

The line between self-defense and attack is sometimes difficult to discern, and using the techniques in this book might have unintended legal consequences. The author is writing as a layman, with no special legal knowledge. Consult with an attorney in your state for advice on the laws about self-defense and attack and the consequencse if you violate those statutes.

Further, the author is not a doctor and has no special medical training. Any information about what the damage a technique can be done with these techniques is merely based on information provided to the author by his ju-jitsu and karate instructors, and not on advice from any doctors. For reliable medical information, contact a physician.

Chapter One

Introduction to the Cane

What else can you carry that is as powerful and useful as the cane, yet still be legal? As long as you claim it is a medical device and not a weapon (which is discussed later in this chapter), it is legal to have it with you. These sticks even go through airport security with no problem. Carrying a cane causes no alarm to the police or opponents.

A cane gives you an extra two to two and a half feet of additional reach to strike somebody with the tip. Or you can swing the cane in an arc to hit (and often break) a bone. Finally, you can hook your opponent's leg or other parts of the body to throw him to the ground. Perhaps most important, a cane doesn't look like an offensive or defensive device. If someone approaches you with evil intent, he will not expect the cane to be a tactical aid and will generally assume you are unarmed.

Fighting with a stick has been around since the days of the caveman. Many countries developed their unique methods of stick fighting. For example, hanbo-jitsu is the Japanese martial art of stick fighting with a straight three-foot staff. As a ju-jitsu instructor in 1961, my grandmaster had an arrangement with the San Francisco Police Department, and trained many police officers. Police officers used the billy club (also called a nightstick or baton) as a street weapon, for both protection and assisting in arresting someone. Billy clubs were eventually phased out in favor of non-lethal devices like pepper spray and tasers. Most of the fifty police departments shown on television during the May June 2020 riots had some officers carrying batons with a side handle (PR-24s).

The club has long been recognized as a formidable aid, and the walking cane deserves this status based on a long history of wooden club use. In many jurisdictions, it is illegal to carry a club, but it is always acceptable to walk with a cane for medical needs. The horned cane (curved handle) is the world's best mobility and personal-protection tool that you can take with you anywhere and at anytime. No other defensive tool is as transportable, versatile, and legal to possess.

The horned cane offers numerous advantages over the straight walking stick. Not only does it fall into a different category legally, but the presence of the horn allows a trained practitioner to perform defensive techniques and maneuvers that are physically impossible to duplicate with a straight stick.

Ability to Use a Cane

Healthy Users

It is easy to understand why young people would gravitate to the cane for self-defense. The cane offers sport, excellent cardiovascular exercise, and formidable self-defense protection.

Mobility-Disadvantaged Users

However, even individuals who must use a cane to walk anywhere can benefit from this device. If someone dependent on a cane fears an attack, he or she can lean against a building to hold themselves steady while using the cane for self-defense.

At worst, if a person is very unsteady, he can sit on a bench, or even just sit on the sidewalk. Sitting so low is not ideal, but few attackers will lean down that far to punch you. An opponents will almost assuredly rely on kicks. That means you need only worry about his legs, and the cane is a strong device to counteract the opponent's mobility and leg strength.

As for wheelchair users, at the end of this book there is a special chapter on defense from a chair.

Regular Canes

Although not truly made for self-defense, a regular wooden crook (rounded handle) will work. However, those canes are thin and not designed for striking, and the crook (handle) is generally too narrow to hook a leg for a throw. Still, they can be effective and are useful for practicing your moves. I've never tested one of those canes but I think they will accomplish their purpose for at least a couple of strikes.[1]

Other canes, like the T-handle and the Fritz-handle, are challenging to use in self-defense because of their straight handles. The typical off-set cane (which looks something like a question mark) is even harder to use. Still, they can be used in a much more limited fashion for self-defense. However, because you will be defending yourself, buy the crook (curved handle) cane. If you can afford it, purchase a specialized self-defense cane.

Fn. 1. I have never tested the strength of ordinary walking canes sold in most pharmacies, but I would expect them to be mediocre to poor in a self-defense swing. Such canes are made for longitudinal strength (i.e., flexural strength, bend strength, or modulus of rupture), which is pressure applied perpendicular to the length of the cane before it breaks. These canes are so inexpensive ($9 to $13), that I am not even sure if they are made of pressed wood particles or natural wood.

It is hard to judge flexural strength without specific tests, because applying the perpendicular pressure at the last third of the cane would give you a different reading than employing that same pressure at exactly the half way point on the shaft. Additionally, the longer the length, the less strength it might take the break the shaft. Some inexpensive canes might be made of real wood, say pine or other softwood. If you can afford it and are serious about self-defense, I recommend purchasing a dedicated self-defense cane.

Self-Defense Canes

When I talk about a cane for self-defense, I mean a cane specifically built for street fighting. A good self-defense cane weighs nearly twice as much as a regular store-bought walking cane. It is usually one-inch diameter round (although, some horned-handle canes can range from 7/8 inch to 1 1/8 inch round). It is made of hardwood, like hickory or oak. Some are even made from metal. The disadvantage of a true-self dense cane is that they are expensive ($80 to $200 or more). However, if you want a unique, solidly-made cane designed for defense, these canes are worth the price.

You can buy self-defense canes on the Internet. Just search for "self-defense canes to buy." You can also find self-defense canes on Amazon.com. I think the best self-defense canes are made by Cane Masters (https://canemasters.com/). Another well-respected source is American Cane Self Defense (https://americancaneselfdefense.com/product-category/canes/).

The Law Regarding Weapons

General Law

As to what the law allows in self-defense, it varies from state to state. If you want a useful reference, see my book, *Defend Yourself with Ju-Jitsu and Karate and Stay Out of Jail*. Or better yet, seek the advice of a local criminal defense attorney.

I am retired and no longer an attorney, so this information is just my layman's opinion. Still, the material below may be helpful.

As long as you claim the cane is for medical purposes,

it should be acceptable to police officers. The minute you claim you use the cane as a self-defense "weapon," you will likely have legal problems. You might want to get a doctor's note or a prescription from a chiropractor stating you need a cane for medical purposes.

Cane Card

If you do not wish to bother your doctor, Cane Masters makes a laminated card (below) that fits in your wallet. The card states that you have the legal authority to carry a cane as a medical device, a right not to disclose your medical condition, and the FAA's permission to take a cane on airplanes. As of this writing, it is $10 at Canemasters.com. It is produced with the permission of CaneMasters, headquartered in Boca Raton, Florida.

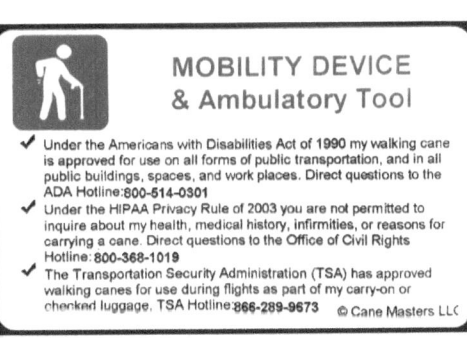

Even though you might have the legal right not to discuss your illness or injury, you must weight that right against the unpleasantness that may result if you refuse to disclose anything to the police. All you need to say is that you use the cane for stability and mobility. Never mention the word "self-defense."

Remember, a cane has many purposes besides just support as you walk. You may need it for help getting up if you fall or as an assistive device for climbing curbs. You may need it in case you encounter uneven sidewalks in your neighborhood. If you claim it is for medical purposes, I would think it would be hard to prove "intent," a required element of most criminal cases.

> Never tell to the police your cane is a weapon. Always refer to it as a medical device. When asked you might want to say something like:
>
> "I carry the cane to help me walk. When he attacked, I was able to use my medical device to help protect myself. He stated he was going to do me great harm. I'm glad my medical cane helps me defend myself. I was scared the whole time he was going to seriously injure me."

Medical Device

Federal law classifies a cane as a medical aid and not as a weapon. "A cane is a device intended for medical purposes that is used to provide minimal weight support while walking." 21 CFR 890.3075. ("CFR" is the abbreviation for the Code of Federal Regulations.)

Wikipedia defines an assistive (normal walking) cane as a medical device to "help redistribute weight from a lower leg that is weak or painful, improve stability by increasing the base of support, and provide tactile information about the ground to improve balance. In the US, ten percent of adults older than 65 years use a cane."

Weapon vs. Medical Device

Almost every cane instructor will emphasize the fact, already mentioned several times in this chapter because it is so important, that you must describe the cane as a medical device and not as a weapon. This is not a law book, but perhaps having a bit more background on the law will help you understand a definition of a weapon. (You can skip this short section if you don't like legal information.) The following is a description of California law, which is typical.

> California Penal Code 22210. "… any person in this state who… or possesses any leaded cane, or any instrument or weapon of the kind commonly known as a billy, blackjack, sandbag, sandc-lub, sap, or slung-shot, is punishable by imprisonment in a county jail not exceeding one year or imprisonment…."

> Court Interpretations. The California Supreme Court stated, "Applying this test to the instant case, we find the possession of the altered baseball bat, taped at the smaller end, heavier at the unbroken end, carried about in the car, obviously usable as a 'billy,' clearly not transported for the purpose of playing baseball, violates the statute. We recognize that the presence of suspicious circumstances attendant to possession of the proscribed object does not forge an ironclad case against defendant. He may be able to demonstrate an innocent usage of the object

but the burden [of proof, or at least proving a reasonable doubt] falls upon him to do so."

And later in the case, the Supreme Court stated, "Thus we hold that the statute embraces instruments other than those specially created or manufactured for criminal purposes... The concomitant circumstances may well proclaim the danger of even the innocent-appearing utensil. The Legislature thus decrees as criminal the possession of ordinarily harmless objects when the circumstances of possession demonstrate an immediate atmosphere of danger.

Accordingly the statute would encompass the possession of a table leg, in one sense an obviously useful item, when it is detached from the table and carried at night in a 'tough' neighborhood to the scene of a riot. On the other hand, the section would not penalize the Little Leaguer at bat in a baseball game." (Emphasis added) *People v. Grubb* (1965) 63 Cal.2d 614, 621.

Author's Advice

The following is my advice, and while I feel it is advisable, it is not mandatory. Also, in some cases there may not be enough time to follow it.

As the police have discovered in 2019 and 2020, there are so many people with cell phones that you should not be surprised if you are filmed during the altercation. If it comes to a jury trial, do you want to be seen as an aggressor or defender?

Here is one way to ensure that you are seen as the defender. Assuming you have time, drop into the ready position for a swing (described in chapter 5), and hold up your other hand in the "stop" position. Now loudly tell the potential attacker: "STOP.... GET AWAY.... GET BACK.... BACK OFF." Anyone in the area will later attest that you were warning the attacker to stay away. In short, you want8 make sure that if called during a jury trial, the witnesses will categorically state that you tried to avoid the fight and urged the attacker to back off.

Shillelagh

Beware of the canes that are sold as shillelagh (pronounced she-LAY-lee). Wikipedia defines these rods as "a wooden walking stick and club or cudgel, typically made from a stout knotty blackthorn stick with a large knob at the top. It is associated with Ireland." In Ireland, and maybe among supplies sold in the States, the large end is sometimes hollowed out and replaced with lead.

The danger of owning or using a shillelagh might depend on the state. I know in California they *would be classified as a weapon*, and I imagine so in many other states. Shillelaghs are normally thought of as weapons and not walking sticks. As one website that sells shillelagh states, "These are made for stick-fighting or personal protection and are not usually comfortable to use as walking sticks."

The Danger of a Cane

As I made clear in the disclaimer at the front of this book, a cane can be a dangerous, even lethal. (You might want to re-read that section.) Depending on where you strike and how hard you hit, you can break bones, damage internal organs, and even kill someone. Since I am not a doctor, this book does not attempt to warn you of the damage that can be done by cane strikes.

Making a Cane

This short section really has nothing to do with self-defense, but I always wondered how you bend a thick stick to make a cane's crook (curved handle). After some Internet research, I discovered most canes start as a one-inch-diameter oak or hickory dowel. Of course, you could use other hardwood or different thicknesses.

You steam the wood for a specified period, depending on the amount of wood being processed. Most manufacturer's use professional steamers, but it can be done in a homemade chamber with a hole for steam like a tea kettle has. Once the wood is done steaming, you use a machine or strong arms to bend the crook to the correct circle size. Then you tie the wood and allow it to dry for several days. When it is fully dry, the crook will remain stable and sturdy. You then sand and coat the rod. I'm always amazed that such a thick, sturdy piece of wood can be bent so easily.

Pronouns

For simplicity's sake, I refer to the attackers using the pronoun "he" and "him" but the attacker could just as easily be a woman. Never make any assumptions on the street about who might attack you, especially if you look wealthy, elderly, or inattentive to your surroundings.

I also assume for simplicity sake your attacker is right-handed. Obviously, some attackers are left-handed.

Parts of a Cane

To study the cane, you need to define your terms. There are four terms which you need to know to understand the instructions used in this book.

Crook
Shaft
Horn
Tip

There may be schools and instructions that may use other synonyms for the above terms.

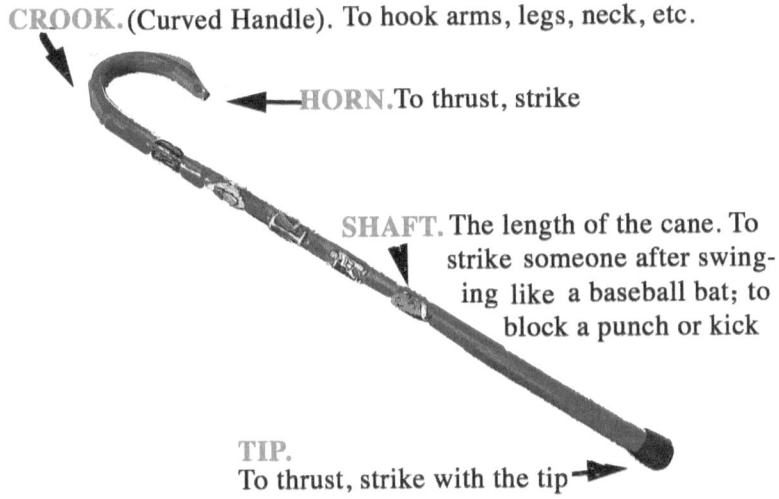

CROOK. (Curved Handle). To hook arms, legs, neck, etc.

HORN. To thrust, strike

SHAFT. The length of the cane. To strike someone after swinging like a baseball bat; to block a punch or kick

TIP.
To thrust, strike with the tip

Many self-defense canes have groves and teeth on one side of the cane. Usually, the outside facing outward is smooth, as you would expect of a cane. But the inside can have a narrow (perhaps one-eighth of an inch) grooves along part of the cane's length. These grooves make the cane easier to grip if you are sweating, or if your opponent tries to pull the cane away from you. The grooves also allow a tighter grip around the shaft of the cane. Some canes have what are called "shark's teeth" on the inside. They vaguely resemble the teeth of an animal and are designed to rub and break opponent's skin, causing more severe injury.

Remember that you "HOOK with the crook, and HIT with the horn."

It is always best to walk with the cane with the horn facing forward, as this properly aligns your forearm over the shaft of the cane—the striking edge of the cane is as shown above. In the horn forward position the striking side of the cane is always facing forward and quickly available for defense using a series of reverse strikes.

The Correct Size

Usually, you buy a cane and cut the tip down to the correct size. Put the crook side of the cane on the ground, near your leg. Hold your arms naturally down at your sides. Immediately above your wrist, you have a protruding bone on each side of your arm. (The radius bone is on the thumb side of your arm, and the ulna bond on the other side.)

Have someone mark the cane where those bones hit on the cane. This measurement results in about a fifteen-degree bend of your wrist when you are walking with the proper sized the cane. For most people, the proper scane size as related to height is approximately as follows:

Person's Height	Cane Size
64" to 67"	35"
68" to 71"	36"
72" to 75"	37"

Umbrella as Cane

When it rains, some people (myself included) carry a reinforced metal umbrella that also functions as a walking stick. Such umbrellas are so strong that they are sold as a self-defense assist, and might, for some people, be considered a worthwile investment. I use the "Unbreakable Umbrella," but there are many other brands on the market. I suggest researching on the Internet before making a purchase.

Don't Look Like a Victim

Introduction

One of the essential elements of safety is to look self-assured and aware of your surroundings. Most people who are attacked look timid and easily intimidated., or appear so distracted by their cellphone or music devices that they cbecome an easy target.

I never practiced criminal law, but attorneys in my office did, and over the years, I talked to many criminals in our waiting room. They all told me the same story. The criminals expected eventually to be caught because the longer you engage in criminal activity, the greater the risk becomes. They all picked victims who were timid-looking people or so distracted that they would be unaware of their approach. Criminals choose easy "marks" because alert and formidable-looking people increase their chance of getting caught. Putting it bluntly, this is a risk-rewards game, with the individual evaluation and decision to attack made in less than 60 seconds. (The exception is someone high on drugs and not reasoning.)

Grayson Study

There is a significant study done in 1981 by sociologists Grayson and Stein, entitled "Attracting Assault: Victims Nonverbal Cues." The study took place in New York, where the sociologist filmed numerous women walking during the day. The videos were shown to rapists and murderers in prison, who were then asked to pick which woman they felt would most likely to be attacked.

Almost all the inmates picked the same women from the vast array of people. And all of them could tell within seven seconds whom they would have selected as a likely victim.

Many signs indicate that a person would make a good target. The three most significant factors are posture, stride, and gaze.

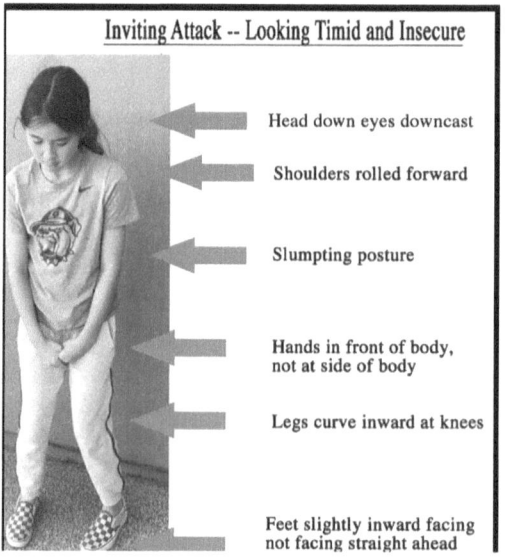

1. <u>Posture</u>. Posture is easy to understand. If a person is bent, with rounded shoulders, and looking down, he or she appears as a victim. In other words, for safety, you should walk with your back straight and your head up. The cliche´ of practicing walking with a book balanced on your head actually illustrates the kind of carriage you need.

2. <u>Stride</u>. The length and speed of a person's

stride were factors is being a victim. The average person walks at a moderately brisk pace, keeping up with any pedestrian traffic nearby. Walking too slow, or unusually fast, it telegraphs insecurity. Therefore, you want to walk at a regular pace, with a smooth and ordinary step, arms swinging naturally.

3. <u>Gaze</u>. The last significant indicator is your gaze. Don't walk with a downward gaze, looking at the ground. Similarly, don't stroll preoccupied with something in your hand. Keep your gaze straight ahead, level with your posture, and briefly scanning the sides and your path. This way, you can't be surprised by someone. If you see a stranger approaching, glance at him, holding his gaze for a few seconds, so he knows you've seen him, then move your gaze elsewhere so as not to appear challenging.

4. <u>Isolation</u>. There is one other factor, not part of the study, but a vital element in your risk of being attacked. The assailant does not want witnesses, so he looks for isolation. If you walk alone in an alley unseen by others, stride by a grove of trees in a park where anyone can grab and hide you, or meander down a poorly lit street at midnight, your risk factor has risen significantly.

Self-defense is more than just having an effective device or usable knowledge. Keep in mind our goal is to not become injured. Therefore, if you can avoid dangerous situations, you are far ahead in protecting yourself. For example, if you see a person or group ahead of you and have a gut feeling they might be trouble, consider turning around and walking the other way. Why face a potential confrontation?

There are a great many things you can do to minimize the risk of dangerous situations. You can never be 100% free of danger, but you can reduce the risks. One of the important goals is to look alert and be aware of your surroundings.

One of my books, "Escape Being Raped or Attacked" has chapters on reducing danger on the street, in your home, at work, in garages, on public stairs, and in many other situations. Alternatively, you can easily Google such phrases as "how to protect yourself from danger" and "how to avoid dangerous street situations."

Goal of a Fight

Your primary goal in a fight is to escape uninjured. Too often, people mistakenly believe they must throttle the opponent so severely that he can never walk again. No, the goal is your safety and survival. If you can walk or run away, you will be uninjured.

Remember, your goal is your safety, not the attacker's punishment. If you must fight, and you knock your attacker to the ground and can safely disengage and retreat, you gain nothing by staying and inflicting more damage.

As I mentioned earlier, under the law, the right to claim self-defense is limited to your defense. If you continue beyond what is reasonable and necessary for your defense, you might face civil and criminal charges. Talk to an attorney or read a book on self-defense law when you begin studying the cane. If you know the use of the cane, but not the law governing its use, you are only half-trained.

Warm-ups

Before you do extended practice with the cane, you would be well advised to first warm-up. The book *The Art and Science of Stick Fighting* has the best discussion I've found on the importance of warm-ups. Joe Varady covers the topic in just three sentences.

> There are more than 10 million sports injuries every year, but many of them could be avoided by implementing a proper warm-up. This produces a two-to three-degree rise in core body temperature that can last for up to 45 minutes, preparing your muscles for strenuous activity and helping to prevent injury… The amount of exercise needed to get to this point varies depending on your cardiovascular conditioning level, but it is recommended that you exercise until you observe light to mild sweating in normal ambient conditions.

Develop a New Habit

If you want to protect yourself, it is essential that you have both hands empty. You can't very well wield a cane if one hand is holding a lawyer's briefcase, a doctor's handbag, a student's canvas case, a shopper's bag of groceries, and so on. If your goal is to protect yourself at all times, then you need to change your habits.

Use a backpack. Your books, medical bag, laptop computer, and other items can go in the knapsack. If you must walk with groceries, use a wheeled cart of some kind. If attacked, you can either walk away from the cart or, if it is sturdy enough, use it as a barrier between you and the attacker.

If you walk into a public garage to climb into your car, have your car key out and in your non-dominate hand (statistically, probably your left hand). Have your cane in your right hand. Keep alert and keep looking around as you walk to your car. In summary, you never know when you will be attacked, and you must change your habits, so you have both hands free.

Summary

Some attacks are just a crimes of opportunity when a criminal suddenly finds a victim in a dark alley or isolated spot. Thus, you cannot avoid all risk, but you can significantly reduce your chance of being attacked.

The following is a true story. One student asked me, "If someone is ten feet away, and she shoots you, what do you do?" I looked at him, smiled, and said, "All black-belts know how to dodge bullets." "Really?" he replied "I'm truly amazed." At this point, I looked him in the eyes and said, "No, you idiot. I'm going to fall to the ground bleeding from bullet holes."

Martial arts give you a substantial advantage, but they don't make anybody invincible. Be realistic in your approach. The cane can be powerful when used for self-defense, but it is only a device that is as good as its user. As one great master said, "The fight that you always win is the one you can walk away from."

The marines teach their soldiers that if they are captured or in the field without a knife or gun, they should use a stick. It is considered the third-best advantage for a marine. They break apart a chair for the leg, rip a branch from a tree, or otherwise obtain a stick to use. As author M. D. Echanis said in his book, Special Forces/ Ranger-UDT/ Seal Hand-to-Hand Combat/Special Weapons/ Special tactics Series:

> The stick is probably the most available 'field expediency' weapon to which a soldier has access, and as a combat weapon it becomes usable for everything from riot control, prisoner control, to an extremely lethal close-quarter combat weapon.
>
> When used properly, the baton [or cane] is one of the most effective tools of control available in man's arsenal of hand-held weapons.

Canes also off a first line of defense against a dog attack. Some people believe there will be more crime on the streets. They cite the June 2020 Federal Reserve ("Fed") projection of near-zero interest rates for probably two more years and high unemployment, especially for businesses that rely on human contact. The Fed projects the permanent loss of millions of U.S. jobs from the Covid-19 virus. in late 2020, banks and credit card companies were making fewer loans and lowering credit limits. Whether the forecast will be accurate or not, you may feel safer carrying a cane.

The footnote below discusses why you medically use a cane on the opporiate side of the body. If you're not interest, skip this note.[1]

Fn 1
Some users will be medically dependent on the cane, and they still want to protect themselves. If you have a sore hip or knee, let's say your right knee, reduce the pain and pressure on your right side, and use the cane on the opposite side of the body. You will be holding the rod in your left hand. Conversely, if you are using the staff for balance and stability, you are better off using it in your less dominant hand. In other words, if you're right-handed, hold the cane in your left hand. Your quicker and stronger right arm is open to break falls or protect against objects in your way.

Medically, you hold the cane on the opposite side of your body; you need to think about the dynamics of walking. Assume your right knee is arthritic, and the goal is to reduce painful

Footnote 1 Continued

downward pressure on that knee. When you step forward with your right leg, you lift your leg off the ground. There is no pressure on the knee while it is airborne. As you step forward with your right leg, all your weight goes to your good left leg. As you step, you move the cane forward with your left hand. Your knee and the cane should come down simultaneously, so the stick can take some of the weight off the bad right leg. Intuitively, this may seem a little awkward, but your body know better. When you walk with two good legs and step forward with your right foot, your opposite arm, the left, usually swings forward.

Your body works in conjunction with other muscles. The arm holding the cane utilizes the back muscles (Latissimus dorsi), which help engage the pelvis and the side hip muscles (gluteus medius). The stick takes the weight, and that stress is distributed to large muscles on that side of the body.

Chapter Two

Situational Awareness

I urge you practice situational awareness (discussed below) and proper attitude (discussed in the last chapter, especially in the Grayson Study). In that case, I believe you will be half as likely to face an attack. Up to half is an incredibly significant reduction in risk factors.

Risk vs. Consequences

When I explained situational awareness in one class, a woman said that she was a runner, and she ran the same path every morning at 7:30 am. Then she took her cane, bent over like a 105-year-old woman, and took a series of half-steps, using the rod with each short stride. "I'm not hobbling along with a cane like this," she said. "I'd never get any exercise."

I told her to stand up straight, and instead of using the cane perpendicular to the ground, carry it in one hand horizontally. I then reiterated that you never know when you will be attacked. If you are without a weapon during an altercation, you must use your hands. Then I suggested she visit a rape center and see how many broken lives never recover from rape and assault. Their life is irrevocably altered for many victims, and they never return to their former outlook on life. It can affect someone's marriage or potential marriage partners, their enjoyment and trust of people, and so many other factors. In short, are the momentous consequences worth the low-to-medium probability? That's your decision.

Internalize the Consequences

Whenever I teach a class, I always have the feeling that some of the students hear me but haven't accepted or internalized how devastating are the long-term consequences of a rape or attack. For most people, an attack leaves a life-long effect. Please try to imagine how severe an attack would be to you. If you can't mentally conjure an image, it will be harder for your "sixth sense" (discussed below) to develop.

Chanel Miller wrote a letter in 2016, which she read into the court record. She was the victim of the well-publicized rape by Brock Turner, a Stanford University student. Am I overly dramatic in providing an example of what I wrote above? Absolutely not! I am trying to penetrate to your brain the severe consequences of a rape or a violent attack. A few paragraphs of Chanel Miller's statement explain how her attack has affected her life:

> "My damage was internal, unseen, I carry it with me. You took away my worth, my privacy, my energy, my time, my safety, my intimacy, [and] my confidence… My independence, natural joy, gentleness, and steady lifestyle I had been enjoying became distorted beyond recognition. I became closed off, angry, self deprecating, tired, irritable, empty. The isolation at times was unbearable. You cannot give me back the life I had before that night either.
>
> I used to pride myself on my independence, now I am afraid to go on walks in the evening, to attend social events with drinking among friends where I should be comfortable being. I have become a little

barnacle always needing to be at someone's side to have my boyfriend standing next to me, sleeping beside me, protecting me. It is embarrassing how feeble I feel, how timidly I move through life, always guarded, ready to defend myself, ready to be angry.

You have no idea how hard I have worked to rebuild parts of me that are still weak. It took me eight months to even talk about what happened. I could no longer connect with friends, with everyone around me."

There are just as many stories from physically attacked or robbed people and suffered post-traumatic stress disorder after the event. Please don't go through your life thinking it can't happen to you so you can let your guard down.

Situational Awareness

Situational awareness is observing your surroundings, analyzing the data received and acting accordingly in a reasonable manner. It is somewhat similar to Colonel Boy's OODA Loop, used by armed services across the globe.

Observation

Observation is different from seeing. Often when you see something that doesn't catch your eye, you can't recall that object ten seconds later. It hasn't registered on your brain. Observation is looking at something with an intent to understand that subject. If you see a man standing near the corner of a building, you don't gloss over that fact. You need to observe that fact, in detail, so you can later analyze it in step two.

One way to improve your observation skills is to take a pen and tablet of paper and look around. Then close your eyes for 10 seconds. Now write down everything you can remember seeing. When you are done, please take a second view, and add it to your list. If you do this process enough times, you find the training allows you to process a great deal of information. Significantly, you will eventually do so without effort on your part. It will become second nature.

Analyze the Data

Now that you have received the data, you must train your mind to process it. Let your mind add all the factors and give you feedback on the conclusion. The strange man near the building, does he look out of place? Are his jacket and attire appropriate, his demeanor reasonable? Are other people nearby, and does it look like a safe place? What are alternatives available to you? (These questions will mean more after reading the paragraphs below on "sixth sense."

Act Reasonably

Once you draw a conclusion, don't ignore your analysis. If the situation doesn't feel right, don't say to yourself, I'm silly; it must be OK to proceed. You must train yourself to look intelligently at your analytical results. Don't let your feeling overwhelm your reasoning. Don't say, the man at the corner will think I'm silly if I turn around and go the other way. Other times, your conclusion may be that it looks safe to proceed, and there is no need to alarm me. Only you can judge but do so with an analytical mind.

Similarly, when you enter a restaurant, a crowded room, a movie theater, get in the habit of noticing where the exits are located. If a fire started, a shooter appeared, or some other emergency happened, how would you get out of the building. Each second counts. If you observed the potential exits when you entered the room in your situational awareness, you are in a far better position.

Sixth Sense

The "sixth sense" is information obtained other than input from the five available organs (sight, touch, taste, smell, and hearing). My definition is more intuitive. It is hearing and trusting that little voice in the back of your mind that warns you of danger. Your logical intellect tells you there might be trouble ahead, but your feelings too often overwhelm your mind.

There is nothing magical going on here. Instead, the data you received from your senses don't seem appropriate, and it warns that you may be entering a risky situation. Remember, analyze and interpret data through the filters of your life experiences, perception of the world, and expectations. So, you never have a perfect analysis of the input from your senses. You are analyzing imperfect data and drawing the best conclusions possible at the time. Use your intuition and learn to trust your instincts. Or, as some people say, "trust your gut."

Ask many victims after rape or attack, and they will often tell you, "That sneaky SOB came out of nowhere." Yet, while he may not have brazenly advertised his presence, there were minor telltale signs that an observant person could have picked up on in most cases. True, you may not have predicted the actual attack, but your senses might have perceived a danger. While you were oblivious to your surroundings and ignored all the subtle indicators, the attacker could close in on you undetected.

Develop Your Sixth Sense

Researchers found that elephants are extra-ordinarily quick to sense danger and react to it. Many animals, including domesticated dogs and cats, can often analyze and see a dangerous situation approaching long before a human can respond. You may never become as quick as other species to recognize danger, but you can train yourself to create situational awareness far faster and with greater accuracy. The military, police forces, and many other organizations train their members to become more situationally aware of their surroundings.

In my ju-jitsu school, our instructors had us look at everyone we saw on the street for two weeks. During that time, we were to imagine every observed person was dangerous and who would attack us. Did he look threatening or meek and unlikely to fight hard? Would you expect him to throw punches, or did he seem like wrestling was more his style? Was he right-handed or a lefty? Are his hands in his pockets, or are they ready to strike? Then, in our minds, we needed to visualize how we would defend ourselves. After two weeks, we were much quicker at recognizing potential danger. More importantly, we maintained an upgraded awareness that required no conscious effort. In other words, we didn't need to walk around thinking, "what if."

Too much awareness can make you paranoid. I don't know if it is true, but I heard one psychiatrist on TV say that one reason soldiers have PTSD (post-traumatic stress disorder) is that they have lived too long on high alert. Now that they are safe, these warriors can't return to normal because they are still stuck on elevated battlefield awareness. In summary, you need to elevate your situational awareness skills. Still, you learn to use them in a more normal way unless something doesn't seem right, and you have instantly snapped into heightened sensitivity.

Practice Scenarios

There is an often-used quote from the ancient Japanese swordfighters, that "the sword cannot go where it hasn't been before. "Modernizing that quote, it would read, "the body can't go where it hasn't been before." In other words, if you haven't practiced the technique, defense, or situation before, normally, you can't do it in an emergency. Your body is drenched with adrenaline and norepinephrine, the fight-flight hormones. You can't achieve what you haven't practiced.

Have a friend act like an attacker and practice using your cane in defenses. Next, go outside and practice on streets, near buildings, open ground, stairs, and various locations.

Chapter Three

Strikes

There are four general types of defensive maneuvers you can execute with a cane. You can jab (thrust) with the cane like a sword, hitting someone with the cane's tip. You can swing the cane and whack him, usually on an arm or leg. You can hook him with the crook of the cane, generally as part of a throw or joint lock. Finally, you can use the shaft to block an opponent's strike or kick. (Blocks are discussed in the next chapter.)

Strike

A strike is hitting someone with the cane using either a jab or a swing. It is a generic term meaning you clobber somebody with the tip of the cane like a sword jab or you slash at an opponent as if the cane were a knife blade.

Jab

Nature of a Jab

A jab is thrusting the cane forward and hitting your opponent with the tip. Many of these techniques were developed long ago using a French foil or slender stabbing sword. Although you can hold the cane with two hands and jab, as soldiers did with a bayonet on the end of their rifle, most jabs are executed with one hand. One-handed jabs are faster but less powerful than two-handed jabs. However, a one-arm strike leaves your other hand free to defend a punch, gab, block, or chop.

Two Motions Involved

Assume your attacker is moving forward, say for a punch, and before he throws that attack, you jab him in the stomach with the cane. The first motion is your strong thrust. All the force generated is transferred to the tip of the cane. If the point is one inch in diameter, all that force is focused on that small one-inch area of the attacker's body. The second motion is his forward momentum impaling himself on your cane tip.

Don't Move Your Shoulder

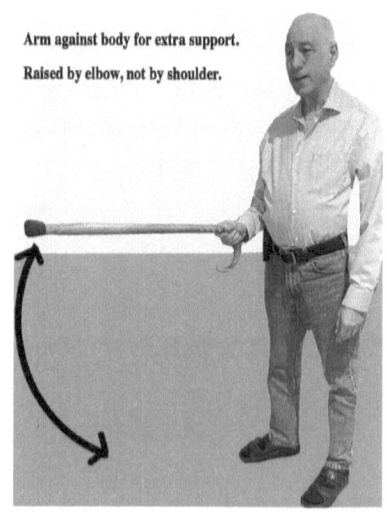

Strike with one hand, using the elbow as your fulcrum (pivot) point. Moving your shoulder would telegraph your move, lessen the intensity of your jab, and, most important, take too long. Just pivot from the elbow.

If you raise your shoulder, then when you step forward or back to thrust the point into your opponent, there is nothing behind your jab but your flapping elbow. Keep your shoulder tight to your body, and you can jab with the full power of your body.

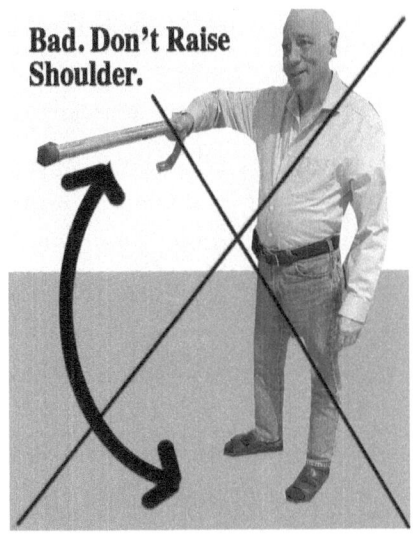

Bad. Don't Raise Shoulder.

Body Supports Strike

When you strike, lock your elbow next to your body. If you are not in a strong stance, step back (or forward) into a forward position. This allows your legs and body to absorb the attacker's momentum pushing back on the cane. Note how the force of an opponent hitting the cane is redistributed through my body. My arm is next to my body so that the arm and body can as much as possible be a single unit.

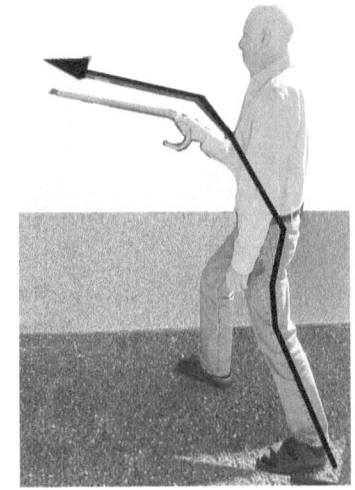

On Jabs Stand Perpendicular

When you jab with the cane, you naturally expect some resistance from your opponent's body. When you jab, you should be standing and step into a stance roughly perpendicular to your assailant. The reason has to do with the physics of resistance.

If I take a book and stand it on its side facing me, I can push it over effortlessly by touching the top. On one occasion I simply blew hard on the top, and the book fell to the table (although I cheated, because it was a paperback and not a hardback). It short, it takes very little energy to push the book over. (See the picture below on the left.) Go ahead and try this.

Now turn the book perpendicular to you and try to push it over. It takes many times more energy to flop the book to the ground. (See the picture on the right.) The same principles apply to you and how you stand. You can absorb an opponent's counterweight when you stand at ninety degrees, but not when you are parallel to your opponent.

Aim for Pressure Points

Ideally, you will hit a pressure point on your opponent's body (discussed in another chapter), where the pain will be multiplied many times over. Examples of typical pressure points are the groin and below the Adam's apple. Thus, for example, if your assailant steps forward with a punch, you can thrust the cane, with its extra two feet of reach, toward his throat. It may be challenging to jab the cane directly into his throat just below his Adam's apple, but if you hit him hard enough, the pain is so great that he will immediately crumple to the ground in agony.

Swing

Swing a Cane

Where you start your swing depends on where the cane is in relation to your body. If the tip sits on the ground in a normal walking cane position, then your swing might begin there. If you have just finished a cane twirl, the crook might be facing forward in your hand, with the shaft parallel to the ground and the tip tucked under your arm. Conversely, you may have cocked the cane over your shoulder, somewhat akin to cocking a baseball bat with one hand. You usually (but not always) swing one-handed, but you can do it from various locations.

You give almost no warning. You raise the cane from your elbow without telegraphing your quick, fast move. Then, without any cocking (back-swing), you swing a hard, fast strike. You aim about three inches inside the person's body or within the area you are striking.

Once you reach your target point three inches inside his body, you quickly stop, without any follow-through. You withdraw the cane as fast can you can, hopefully near the speed of your initial strike. You return to your ready or on-guard position.

Not a Baseball Swing

Some beginners assume swinging the cane is like swinging a bat in baseball. Baseball is quite different. It is helpful first to break down a baseball swing so you can visualize the difference. In baseball, you place two hands on the bat near the handle; your dominant hand is on top; the knuckles of each fist aligned in a row. The bat lies over your rear shoulder at about a forty-five-degree angle to the ground. You stand at the plate perpendicular to the pitcher, with your non-dominant foot forward. Your lead foot takes a small step as you swing from the shoulders, then the hips, and finally the knees. You follow through so the bat ends up on the other shoulder.

Number and Types of Strikes

There are eight possible strikes. You can swing horizontally (left to right or right to left) or vertically (top to bottom or bottom to top). Finally, you can swing diagonally (top left to bottom right, top right to bottom left, bottom right to top left, or bottom left to top right).

However, in actual use in the street, since you are holding the cane in your dominant hand, most of the strikes are from your dominant shoulder or from overhead, coming straight down or diagonally down.

Someone did a study of riot police, amateurs, and even trained cane users and found that over 80 percent of offensive swings were diagonal or from overhead. The other 20 percent were mostly instances when the user switched from offense to self-defense to block an opponent's attack or to jab with the cane tip.

Practice with Two Strikes

Unless you are practicing repetitions of the same strike, say twenty-five to fifty overhead strikes, you are better off practicing two-strike combinations. You want to build muscle memory so that on the street you will always be prepared for a second strike. You will then be in a position to deliver the follow-up maneuver if it proves necessary.

Diagonal Strikes

Since this book is assuming you are right-handed, the first basic strike combination is the upper right-left diagonal combination. Cock your right hand, holding the cane near your right ear; then slice downward hard and fast toward your left hip. When your hand

reaches your hip, your cane tip should be near the ground. Quickly raise your right hand to the cocked position, hand near your left ear. Now swing diagonally toward your right hip. Note that on the return strike you turn your hand over so that the return, too, is a powerful strike.

Start slowly, making sure your path is correct and the movement feels easy and accurate. Keep repeating this movement until it becomes second nature. This strike will probably be your most useful tactic.

After you feel you have this technique in your muscle memory, strike at a small target, again starting slowly. You can use a six-inch-long piece of used tire (easy to obtain from any tire dealer, usually for free). I use a six-inch-long rubber tire stop (picture below), but any hard rubber surface will do. After you feel comfortable, increase the speed and power of each part of your diagonal strike as you hit the rubber surface.

Don't smother your strikes; make sure you are taking a full swing. However, you are not marching in a parade, meaning you want the hand holding the cane to stay more or less within the width of your body. This provides a faster recovery, is more powerful, and allows greater control. Develop accuracy by making each strike follow exactly the same path. Speed and power will come naturally over time.

Be sure to practice all the strikes on the right-hand side and then the left-hand side of your body. You need to be equally comfortable with your right hand and your left hand in all combinations.

Power of a Cane

Sped and Recovery

The secret of karate strikes and other martial arts that use chops and punches is the technique in which they are delivered. It is somewhat similar to the power of a whip.[1]

What makes the whip so vicious is the snap at the full potential of the blow. It is followed almost instantly by the quick and speedy recovery of the whip. It is the snake-like in-and-out motion that creates the power. The same idea applies to karate punches.

In breaking a board, you aim about three inches below the bottom of the board. Most of the speed of the punch is reached before the blow is delivered. Once you reach your target point, here three inches below the board, you quickly withdraw your hand as fast as possible.

While boxers' punches can often have the same power as a karate punch, it is an entirely different type of force. A fighter hits the other person and follows through with the blow, not concerned with the speed of the withdrawal. The boxer is trying to mash a part of the body, whereas a karate punch is designed to crack something.

Power Function of Speed

The difference between a beginning karate student and a black-belt instructor is mostly speed and ac-

---

Fn. 1. The sound of a whip cracking is caused by the tip moving so fast that it breaks the sound barrier and creates a small sonic boom. But to produce the crack, the person holding the whip must reverse the whip while it is in motion, so that part of the lash is recoiling in the opposite direction. In other words, it is what one article calls the "cobra-like in-and-out recoil" that allows the whip to reach such speeds. The power from the thick part of the strap and the handle travels to the small tip of the lash. The slender end reaches full acceleration. Then, just as it reaches maximum velocity, it is being withdrawn.

curacy. There is more power, too, in an advanced punch, but the most salient factor is the speed.

Remember high school physics class. Newton's second law, somewhat simplified, holds that force equals mass times acceleration. In other words, the faster you throw a punch, the more striking power it will have. A good cane strike can be five to ten times as fast and powerful as a karate punch.

I remember reading or being told by an instructor (I can't remember which) that it only takes about 250 pounds of force to break a one-inch-thick board. While it is technique, not strength, that breaks the board, even a beginner can crack a one-inch board with minimal training. My grandmaster used to say that breaking a board is easy because the board is not fighting back.

I remember a teenage black belt in our school who easily cracked a one-inch board with the edge of his hand. What was impressive was that he did it beginning with his hand precisely four inches from the board. If I hadn't seen that with my own eyes, I don't know if I would have believed it.

A black-belt expert in a helicopter spin can swing the tip of the cane over two hundred miles per hour, as measured by a radar gun. Therefore, beginners with the proper technique should be able to reach one hundred miles an hour without much problem. At that speed, with a heavy wooden cane, you can do considerable damage to someone, breaking bones and even causing internal organ damage.

At speeds of one hundred miles per hour, it is obvious that your ubiquitous medical device can offer great personal protection, a sense of security, and a feeling of freedom as you walk the streets.

The quick summary of this detailed explanation is that the faster you swing the cane, the more power from your strike. So, when you practice on a heavy bag, the tire device discussed in this book, or a tree, work to develop speed and accuracy at a specific target area.

Danger Zone, Loss of Cane, and Cocking the Cane

Danger Zone

The danger of a cane strike is limited by the length of the cane. Naturally, if you are beyond the reach of the cane, it can do you no damage. If you are between the handle of the cane and the person wielding it, you cannot be hit with the cane. You can still be kicked, punched, kneed, or thrown by the attacker if he knows unarmed combat.

If You Lose Your Cane

Although not technically part of offensive cane work, it is important to know what to do if you lose your cane or it is taken from you. If your attacker swings for your head, the first and safest option is to run away, staying beyond the reach of the cane. The second and riskier option is to rush the attacker and get inside the cane area for a tackle, punch, or knee to the opponent.

Understand, you can dart inside the danger zone. You must close quickly to land in the safe zone—the space between the end of the cane and his arm. The best place is approximately a foot past the tip of the cane. You are safe from its range but close enough to run at the attacker if the opportunity presents itself.

Good cane fighters don't wind up before they strike, but most amateurs do cock their stick over their shoulder before they strike. The moment you see your opponent with your cane pull back his shoulder, winding up for a strike, that is when you completely

commit yourself and rush forward. Have your hands above shoulder height, so you can perhaps block his arms, neutralizing the attack. If you do get hit, it will be your arms instead of your head taking the blow.

If he has already cocked the cane, you are too late to rush. Keep out of the way, and wait until he winds up for the next strike. You are not fast enough to dart into the danger zone once he has begun his swing.

Cock the Cane

While cocking the cane before as part of your strike is not done by experienced used, standing in a cocked position as a warning is often employed. Cocking the cane is similar to cocking a gun. With the stick, you bring your arm back by your ear, ready to unleash a swing at your opponent. If you have time, the most potent offensive strikes originate from the cocked cane position. And as you will learn later, you yell "back away," as you hold this position, so witnesses can testify you didn't initiate the attack if cops are called.

Hook and Crook

Hook

A hook is using the crook (curved handle) of the cane

to capture an arm, leg, neck, or other part of your opponent's body. You then lock that body part down tight or use the hook to throw the person. Of course, the crook is wood, so you could use it for a jab or swing, but I feel the primary use of the cane's handle is for grappling. It can quickly swing out and hook an appendage or wrap around the neck. However, store-bought walking canes have too narrow of a crook to catch most legs or arms or to fit around the neck. So such tactics are limited to self-defense canes.

Crook

At the tip of the crook is the other end of the cane, often called the crook or small end. On a self-defense cane, the end is frequently ground to a narrow point and can be used as a knife to stab parts of the body. Generally, the end is not sharp enough to penetrate like a knife, but the small point focuses so much weight behind it that it can inflict punishing pain when delivered in the right places.

Perfecting Your Techniques

Karate Striking Board

In the 1950s and early 1960s, before martial arts gained popularity in the U.S., karate studios often used what was called a makiwara board to practice striking techniques. "Makiwara" is an Okinawan word that means wrapped ("maki") rope ("wara"). In the U.S., the top was not rope but canvas, covering a four-inch piece of strong foam nailed to the top of the board.

Some Asians used it to develop huge calluses on their knuckles, but in the U.S., it was utilized to perfect the alignment of hand and wrist for hitting a solid surface exactly square on. Hitting it hard developed your ability to gauge the distance of your strike, maximize the speed of your hips, and perfect the correct position of the wrist and fist. You hit with the first two knuckles of your hand, not your whole fist, and the back of your fist is in perfectly straight alignment with your forearm.

Now, instead of makiwara boards, they have three-dimensional hard rubber figures, such as "Bob," that are anatomically correct and more forgiving than a board.

Practice Striking

Most new students begin cane practice by striking the tires as hard as possible. But the goal, as with the makiwara board in karate, is to develop accuracy and technique. Strike slowly, work on perfecting your stance, and only slowly add power to your strikes. The proper technique will allow you to strike more powerfully.

Direction of Strike

As any baseball player can tell you, the key to hitting a home run is hitting the ball on the sweet spot on the bat at exactly a ninety-degree angle to the bat. The same goes for the cane. The most powerful strike is one delivered at ninety degrees to the target, so the full impact is driven into the target. If you strike at an angle, you may deliver only a glancing blow, with the power dissipated over a large target area. As with a karate punch, you don't aim to stop the strike at the surface of the skin. Instead, aim to withdraw the strike from a point two inches or more beyond the surface of the attacker's body.

Making a Cane Practice Device

The general principle of makiwara boards applies to practice with the cane, but you make the device out of tires. There are many methods, but the easiest involves two used tires. Lay the bottom one on a waste sheet of plywood, covered by a plastic sheet or bag. Pour concrete into the tire. Before the concrete hardens, set a three-foot-tall two-by-four board in it, perpendicular to the tire. Once the concrete fully hardens, remove the board and plastic sheet. Now put a tire over the top of the two-by-four and secure it to the board using long machine screws, washers, and nuts.

You can also put two tires on the board, for upper and lower strikes. For an even easier solution, you could just hang a tire from a tree, the same way you make a tire swing for a child.

Alternate Cane Practice Device

Sometimes a sturdy post with an arm sticking out will

serve you well in practicing your strikes and focus. In my den I have a device that is a coat rack, but instead of hooks it has a round dowel sticking out. It allows me to practice my focus, striking, and blocking techniques.

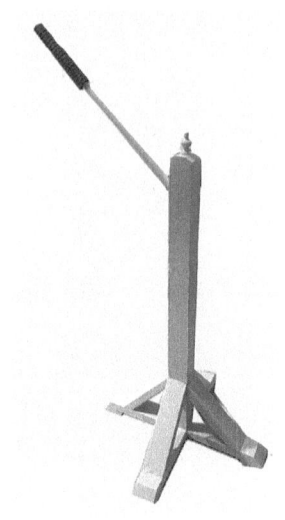

It is easy to make, and the plans are online, with instructions on how to cut the wood (www.shanty-2-chic.com). A picture of my device is below. To secure the round dowel, I used a one-inch-diameter hardwood dowel and drilled in the four-by-four with a one-inch drill at a forty-five-degree angle. Then I drilled through another side and screwed in a thick stainless-steel lag bolt, further securing the one-inch dowel. I wrapped the end of the dowel with half-inch rubberized foam.

Advantage of Muscle Memory

Reacting automatically during an attack, without involving your forebrain, saves precious seconds, giving you a faster response time. Equally important, as you practice a particular block and strike sequence, you perfect your accuracy. To use an analogy, in shooting a pistol, it doesn't matter how many shots you can fire in a ten-second burst if none of the lead hits the target. You need to practice for both accuracy and force, and the more you practice, the faster your cane moves. As I've said so many times in this chapter, speed comes from practice, not from brute force.

Chapter Four

Blocks

If you don't block or otherwise neutralize your opponent's strikes, you will be hit. If you are hit hard enough, you might be so stunned that you can't retaliate. Blocking is of primary importance. Even if you manage to block, but you don't hit back, your opponent will keep attacking until you are disabled.

Most beginning students will tell you that striking is fun, glamorous, and satisfying, and that blocking is boring and unexciting. The criticism relates to mental gratification and has nothing to do with protecting yourself. Protecting yourself is half the battle; it is an essential part of fighting.

The punishment of your opponent is not an aim; your goal is to make him stop attacking. Remember, your goal in street combat is to walk away uninjured. It is NOT to win the fight.

Blocks and Parries

The descriptions and uses of every block could fill this entire book. Your goal is to learn enough blocks to protect yourself without being overwhelmed. As with any basic course, you need effective techniques that will work, but also, more important, that are easy to perfect. Average users can rely on simple but effective blocks in a street fight, and leave the fancy blocks to more advanced users.

Blocks

Nature of a Block. A block is a substantial hit against a punch or kick that disrupts the direction of the attack. You meet force with force. Punches are blocked only below the elbow (the forearm) and kicks only below the knee. (The application of such techniques is covered in a later chapter.) Your block is most often a type of strike, which hopefully damages your opponent and stops the attack.

Inside Block. Most of the blocks you will do are inside blocks, meaning you are parallel to the opponent and hitting his arm to push it away from your respective bodies. You are violently altering the punch to the outside of your opponent's body.

Outside Blocks. Outside blocks are just as effective as inside blocks but require slightly more skill. To perform this maneuver, you must be outside of the attacker's shoulders and hit the punch or kick so that it is forced to travel toward your opponent's center line.

Parries

The difference between a block and a parry is in whether you materially alter the trajectory of an incoming punch or strike. With a block, you meet his blow with a powerful force of your hand, arm, or cane striking his forearm. Conversely, with a parry, you quickly step outside the range of a strike and let that strike pass harmlessly by without significantly disturbing its path. You sometimes hear a parry described as a soft technique. My son, who used to take karate, calls it an invisible block. While your hand or cane is usually near your face as protection, like a protective guard, in most instances you don't even touch the punch. There is no need.

For beginning students, parries are only done to straight punches. It doesn't matter how far away you are from the punch when you do the parry. Sometimes you are within an inch or less of the punch or strike, while other times you may be a foot or more from your opponent.

Blocks with Shaft

Most attacks you face in the street you are punches, although the blocks can be used against weapons and any type of assault. The block has several purposes:

1. **Protect Yourself.** First, of course, is to keep yourself from being hit. If you fail to block an oncoming strike, you will be struck, perhaps hard enough to knock you out of the fight. So the number one priority of a block is to make sure it is effective.

2. **Punishing Block.** Second, you can hope the block with a cane will be punishing enough for the attacker to withdraw. In effect, the block becomes an offensive move in addition to its defensive nature.

3. **Ready for Counterstrike.** Finally, you want to block in such a manner that you are ready for a counterstrike. You want to unleash a powerful strike of your own. As the axiom goes, "The best defense is a strong offense."

Too many students neglect blocking techniques. In my opinion, a full one third of your time should be spent on blocking. You should be so proficient that you can see most attacks coming and have an energetic block ready. Powerful blocks help accomplish the goal of getting the attacker to stop fighting.

1. **Use Body to Power Blocks.** In any block, when you have time and ability, you should be using your hips effectively to augment the block. The stronger the block, the more punishing it becomes. When your hips rotate in the direction of the block, you are utilizing the force of your body to increase your arm's strength in delivering a rock-solid block.

2. **Withdraw the Cane Quickly**. Once you have blocked the attack, quickly withdraw the cane. You gain nothing by leaving it in position and, at worst, risk its being grabbed. The faster you remove the stick, the faster your counterstrike can begin.

3. **Two Types of Blocks**. There are at least two different types of blocks with a cane.

> The first is a swinging block, where you generate the full power of your moving cane, back, hips, and legs driving that swing into his arm or other attacking appendage. My son always likes the analogy of taking a golf club and swinging it full force into an attacker's arm.
>
> The second type of block is a pushing block. You push the cane, usually with two hands, to a position against his attacking arm or leg and hold it steady in that position.

Swinging Block

In a swinging block, you raise the cane to your head (cocking the cane), then forcefully strike down at the attacking fist or kick. As you swing, you can step back or forward, increasing your safety by moving from the strike area.

Sometimes, especially if you are not ready for the strike, you might stay stationary and just block your opponent's attack. Almost all swinging blocks that you will use are one-handed blocks.

Or, of course, you could use the block for a low strike or kick. These blocks are ideal for attacks below the waist, such as a kicking attack. The goal is to practice the bocks until you are comfortable with them and then to select the particular blocking style that works for you.

The same rule that applies to strikes also applies to blocks: Keep your elbows close to your body for support and power. Don't use your wrist as your fulcrum; instead rotate from the elbow.

Don't Raise Shoulders and Elbow

Just as in punching, if you raise the shoulder and elbow significantly, you hinder your block's speed and power. Most of the energy from a block comes from your shoulders and back, plus the acceleration produced by your arm muscles. It is the strong pectoral muscles and back muscles that generate the devastating power of a block. When you raise your elbow and shoulders, you disengage much of your large pectoral muscles' power and decrease your back muscles' dominance. Without those two groups, you lack the strength of your big muscles, and most importantly, you curtail the explosive power of the speed you can generate when you swiftly block your opponent. In short, with your shoulder and elbow raised, you produce more of a pushing motion instead of a fast, snapping motion from dynamic, accelerated motion of your arm augmented by the muscle groups.

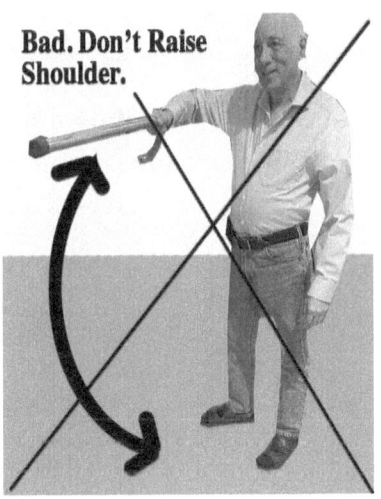

Pushing Block

There is a pushing block that does not rely on acceleration or dynamic action. It is the pushing block, which is a two-handed block, where you raise the cane. With your non-dominant hand, place your palm against the inside shaft. The reason you don't grab the cane with that hand is that if your fingers were wrapped around the cane, they could be hit and smashed. Push from the inside out (or for an outside block, from the outside in).

1.   **Eight Angles of Blocks**. Below is an octagon, which has eight sides. The direction of the cane in push blocks can be in any of the eight different positions.

2.   **Elbows In**. Be sure that when you are pushing to the side (upper side, vertical side, or lower side), your bent elbow is on the opposite side of your body. (See photograph below.) If your bent elbow is on the same side as the block, it will stick out. Such an appealing target is likely to get hit. So don't stick your elbow out.

Wrong. Elbow will get hit. Bent elbow is other side of body.

3. **Horizontal Blocks**. Horizontal blocks over the head are mostly used in protection against other sticks, and for beginner students, it is essential to practice them. However, you seldom need this block. On the other hand, the downward horizontal is occasionally used to block kicks.

 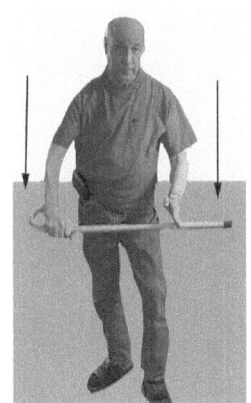

Counterattack

Of course, as soon as you have blocked the attack, you must immediately launch into a counterattack. Any movement that disrupts the attack by deflecting it is a block. (Later chapters will discuss how to use the block against different attacks.)

What Time Is It Attack

According to studies, most people who approach someone to rob them first ask if they have the time. The minute that person looks down at his watch, the assailant attacks. Given that information, I suggest you either tell people you don't know what time it is or keep walking while you answer. Above all, keep your eyes open and don't walk down the street preoccupied with your smartphone or other device.

Chapter Five

Stances and Positions

Stances and cane positions are so important that they deserve a separate chapter. If you aren't ready for an opponent's attack, it becomes harder to move quickly to defense. These positions give you the time and effectiveness you need for a strike. As to stances, no one stance is right for everyone. However, two stances that have proven very effective are the so-called natural stance ("hachiji dachi" in Japanese karate) and a modified back position ("kokutsu dachi").

Fixed Stances

Natural Stance

In the natural stance, the feet are shoulder width apart; the feet are each at about a thirty-five- to forty-five-degree angle to each other. It is a relaxed stance to hold with little muscular exertion. It is also commonly used stance when someone approaches and has not yet shown any aggressive tendencies. It is not considered a fighting stance; you don't usually engage in offensive strikes. You may block from this position.

Back Stance

In the back stance, your dominant foot is in the rear, at about ninety-degree angle to your body, while your front foot is slightly over two feet from the back foot. The front foot is facing forward, and both knees are bent. The feet are shoulder width apart. In karate, 70 percent of the weight is on the rear leg. However, for cane fighting, you want the back leg to have about 60 percent of the load. This is a stance from which you can launch offensive and defensives moves.

One benefit of the back stance is that your vital internal organs are turned away from the attacker, so they are harder to reach. It also rectifies the weakness of facing parallel to the attacker. Remember the example in chapter 3 about how much harder it was to push over the book when it was perpendicular to you.

Flexibility in Stances

In all cases, you want to keep your back straight, eyes straight ahead. When you strike with the cane, you want your hips and back leg to fully support you against any recoil or reverse force from your opponent . In other words, your whole body supports the swing or thrust of your cane.

You have to pick what stances work for you. A boxer will probably maintain his boxing stance and be comfortable with it. You want your knees somewhat bent and your weight roughly equally distributed, or slightly more on the back foot. The main things you want from your stance are stability, flexibility, and the ability to move quickly.

Partially Disabled Stance

If you require the cane for walking and have a weak leg, you will need to assume whatever stance your body will accommodate. You should consult with a doctor on exercises that can strengthen your bad leg. Surprisingly, ten minutes a day of therapeutic exercise for a month can often make a difference in a street fight. You want to be able to laterally step a foot or so without falling while swinging your cane.

Your health or your life may depend on your doing enough exercise that you can take a step and still maintain your balance. Plus, of course, it will help you get around and perhaps reduce future deterioration.

If you can't step and maintain your balance, as was

discussed in the first chapter, you can lean against a building or sit on the ground.

Two Cane Positions

There are two usual cane positions before you strike. The first is the ready position, for when someone is approaching you and you want to appear somewhat relaxed but ready. The second is the on-guard stance, where you are prepared to strike with the cane.

Different schools teach different methods, but in my mind, it all boils down to whether you want to swing the cane in an arc or jab with a thrust of the tip like you would with a sword. Which one you use—swing position, jab position, or holster position—depends on the circumstances, how much trouble you are expecting, and what is most comfortable to you. (The holster position is discussed later in this chapter.)

The Swing Position

Ready Position. As previously discussed, in the ready position, you hold up your non-dominant hand, palm forward, fingers toward the sky, like a policeman signaling traffic to stop. With your dominant hand, hold the cane about chest high, tip pointing toward the sky. Command in a very firm and loud voice, "Stop." Then say, "Back off. Back off." Because your hands are shoulder width apart and open, the stance is slightly less threatening and not wholly aggressive.

On-Guard Position. Here you bring the cane back by your shoulder, just waiting for a need to swing the cane into a body part.

The Jab Position

Ready Position. The ready position is often just the natural stance discussed at the beginning of this chapter.

On-Guard Position. Here you grab the cane in the traditional rifle bayonet ready position. Your dominant hand holds the back of your cane near the handle, knuckles facing up. Your dominant foot is behind. Your other hand grips the cane in about the middle, with the knuckles facing down. The crook is held below waist height, and the hand holding the crook is next to the body.

Note on e hand up, one hand down.

Bottom of cane below waist

The tip of the cane is pointing straight at the opponent's breastbone. In this position you are prepared to jab into your opponent.

Striking from Jab Position. From the on-guard position, you can jab with great power at your assailant's breastbone or throat. You can also act in defense, blocking an attack.

Holster Position

End of Twirl Position. Another chapter discusses twirls. At the end of a twirl, the cane is tucked under your arm. The crook is face up, so that the cane can swing freely from this position. Many call this position holstering the cane, and it is an effective striking stance.

Striking from Holster Position. You can strike from this position merely by swinging the cane in an arc parallel to the ground. It is a very powerful strike.

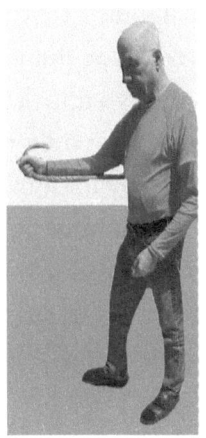  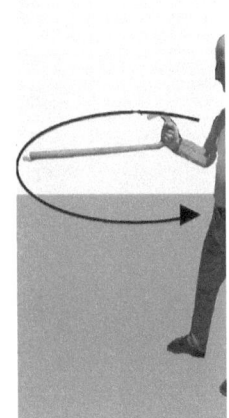

Holding the Cane

When you grip the cane, your hand grabs the cane in the normal grasp, but your thumb should be tucked over your fist. If your thumb is loose, it could become tangled with your clothes or be injured by the attacker. Your grip should be firm, but not so tight as to hurt your hand. If there is too much tension in your grip, it can actually slow down the speed of your strike.

Your empty hand should be in one of two positions. It should be either at about chin level, ready to block or punch as needed, or parallel to your opponent's lead hand (or, if a weapon is involved, his weapon hand). Of course, fighting stances are very specific to the individual. If you are more comfortable having your hand elsewhere, as long as there is a reason for its placement, keep it where it best fits your fighting style. Those who favor a karate or boxing approach will probably keep the empty hand in a fist, while those who prefer a ju-jitsu or wrestling style should keep the hand open, palm facing the opponent.

Walking with the Cane

Not a Game

Some cane owners have a fantasy that an attacker will saunter up from the street, look them in the eyes, and say, "Get ready. I am going to attack you as soon as you are ready." Unfortunately, while most of the time you do have time to be ready for an attack, some violence arises unexpectedly. You must be ready at all times. This doesn't mean you travel down the street fearful with each step. Rather, it means you are always conscious of your surroundings, and your cane is ready to be used at any time. You are relaxed but ready, and your cane is in the best position to spring into action when needed.

Hold Cane Vertically

When you walk along the sidewalk or in a store with your cane, move with the cane perpendicular to the ground. Many practitioners who learn from books carry the cane parallel to the ground, holding it in the middle of the shaft. In this position it takes the user longer to slide the hand to the end of the cane so it can be used effectively.

Reverse Horn to Front

The most effective way of walking with a self-defense cane is to use it like a normal cane, but with the horn (the round handle end) facing forward. Such is the reverse of the way most people normally walk with the cane. There are several benefits of holding the can in this reverse-horn position, but the main advantage is that if you need to raise the cane into a "cocked" position, you can do so without difficulty. Your forearm is properly aligned over the shaft of the cane for a cocked or ready position.

Chapter Six

Figure 8: The Best Move in this Book

Criminals and predators look for "soft targets" and preferably someone older and weaker. Most people using a cane for defense and mobility come to realize that they will likely encounter attackers who are one third of their age and physically superior. The odds are with the attacker in the sense that if it comes to wrestling, you will almost always lose. If you were to learn only a single defensive technique with the cane, it should be the figure 8. Even with limited training, employing the figure 8's cone of protection as you scream your lungs out requesting help may just save your life.

Introduction

Importance

The figure 8 is so important that it warrants its own chapter. It is the most effective defensive move you can employ to "level the playing field" against a bigger and stronger opponent.

In the late 1830s Samuel Colt developed the first modern revolving pistol, and he is remembered for his oft-quoted line "God created men, and Samuel

Colt made them equal." The .45 caliber Colt pistol was later credited with "winning the West" and made disparities in size or physical limitations irrelevant.

Your self-defense cane is a less lethal alternative to a pistol and, with proper training, can play a similar role in your personal protection. In my educated opinion, a good figure 8 will deter most potential attackers. To the potential assailant, you cease to be an easy target and pose too high a risk to be worth attacking.

Of all the cane defenses and techniques in this book, this one movement is probably the most important concept you should learn. Practice the figure 8 technique until it is second nature and you can perform it with either hand.

Spinning Your Cane

Spinning from the Shaft. There are two ways of performing the figure 8: near the top of the shaft or from the crook. When spinning from the upper shaft, you grip the cane about six to eight inches below the crook. This position provides better control and allows you to strike with precision and power. This hand position also offers superior balance and is a launching position for other cane techniques such as moving to a new position quickly. This method of spinning is harder to learn and takes more practice, but once mastered, it is the preferred method of starting the figure 8 spin.

Spinning from the Horn (crook). The second method of swinging figure 8s is done by gripping the cane's crook. While spinning from the horn is less precise than spinning from the shaft, the technique offers at least three positives. First, it is far easier to spin from the crook, and even though it supplies power, it is still more than adequate speed to deter anyone. Secondly, this grip requires (in my opinion) 30 to 50 percent less energy and endurance than spinning from the shaft. For elderly, injured, or infirm users, this may be the only way they can swing the figure 8 for a prolonged period. It is also an easier solution to learn. Lastly, some of the cane techniques, such as the "windshield washer" and "helicopter spin," can be initiated only in the "horn up" position while gripping the crook.

When spinning from the horn (crook), you pivot your wrist, and it becomes your fulcrum point.

I have to sidetrack a little with an analogy. Some instructors will correctly tell you that you can generate 30% to 50% more power spinning from the shaft. True but those percentages only tell half-the story.

I have to sidetrack here a little with an analogy demonstrating how meaningless some numbers can be out of context. The nearest star to our sun is Alpha Centauri, followed by Barnard's Star. The difference between these stars is 8.289 trillion miles, which is such a staggering distance that a million miles here or there is meaningless. Yet a million miles is 126,500 times the diameter of Earth.

Going back to the cane, the speed of the figure-8 web is insignificant to many attackers. True, it will matter when he is hit. However, for an assailant considering whether or not to attack, I suggest the cane's speed is unimportant. Spinning from the horn is still an effective technique, and you should be immediately following up with a second strike

A skilled practitioner should be able to make figure-8 spins from either the shaft or horn and switch between the two effortlessly while maintaining a continuous series of spins. It just take practice!

The Nature of Figure Eight

Effectiveness

The figure-8 spin was designed as a defensive move to use when your life is threatened; it can be used to deter an attack, as well as to defend yourself while being attacked. It helps form a "wooden fence" or "cone of protection" around you that is scary for anyone seeking to do you harm. The move is simple in concept; you make a figure 8 with your cane and keep repeating the movement.

You want to make it seem like a propeller blade. The attacker is deterred when he doesn't see any way to stick any part of his body in the path of your cane without getting hit. The picture below is grossly exaggerated to give an easy-to-understand representation of the technique. In use, the cane never travels far outside your body area.

There are three reasons for keeping your elbows confined to the narrow space between your shoulders. First, you don't have any dangling appendages, such as arms and elbows, to protect, making you a smaller target. Next, the less room you have to cover laterally, the faster your cane can traverse the figure 8. Finally, your strike becomes more powerful when you keep your pectorals, the giant muscles of your upper chest, locked within your body area.

In reality, the figure 8 is so squashed it almost becomes a vertical figure 8, while your elbow stays relatively level on a horizontal plane just below the solar plexus.

Note that while spinning the cane with my dominate hand, my other arm is not hanging at my side. It is in a fist, almost chin high, ready to strike or block if the need arises.

Pre-Practice Maneuvers

The first way to start familiarizing yourself with figure 8 is to hold the cane firmly and move your arm in a figure-8 pattern. Repeat it about twenty times until you are familiar with the configuration. Remember, it is mostly forearm and wrist movement. You don't want to flap your arm like a bird in flight. Your elbow should be tightly tucked into your rib cage. Now repeat the same motion using your other hand. That procedure is not exactly the way to do the process, but it makes learning easier.

Performing the Figure Eight

Establish Figure-8 First

Now practice the spin the correct combat way. Hold the cane firmly in your hand, but allow for a bit of wobble in your grip. The speed and motion are generated by the actions of your wrist, hand, and forearm. Learn the spin first from the shaft. Even though this technique is harder to learn, it will allow you to spin with power, speed, and accuracy.

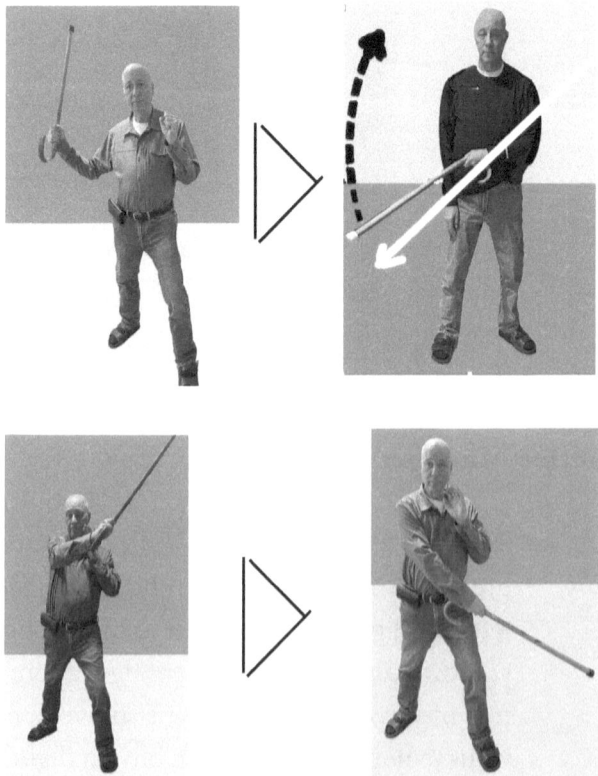

It helps to do hundreds with your right hand and then hundreds with your left, so the movement becomes natural and comfortable from either side. Practice changing hands in the middle of a spinning sequence without breaking rhythm

Power Comes from Speed

As Newton's law states, force equals mass times acceleration. In other words, the faster you spin the cane, the more striking power it will have. Repetition in a correct trajectory allows you to speed up.

Forcing yourself to spin faster before mastering the technique leads to faulty control, slower strikes, and weakened accuracy.

Let repetitions automatically build power. I feel that the best way to practice the figure 8 is to do one hundred spins per day with each hand as a warm-up. Over the months, you will notice the increase in speed and power without sacrificing good form.

Hitting a Stick

For another type of practice, have a friend hold a four-foot stick out in front of you, with the end about one to two feet in front of your chest. Your friend needs the rod's long length to avoid getting hit if you accidentally strike a little off-center. Now do your figure eight, beating the stick each time you do the figure eight. It helps you practice your concentration, adapt to having some resistance during your swing, and develop your accuracy.

Use in Street

Author's Advice

As already mentioned in this book, and because it is so important, the defend method is repeated here, again. When confronted, if you have a chance, drop into the "ready position" and give your "back off, back off" warning. Use a loud voice, as you may need witnesses if you are attacked. If your potential attacker closes the gap, drop into your figure 8 technique, staying directly in front of him.

Maneuvering

If you are being attacked, it is much less desirable to defend yourself from a stationary position. A static position makes it easier for your opponent to strike you, whereas it is much harder for him to strike a moving target.

Skilled practitioners learn how to maneuver the cane as they are moving and switching between a "horn up" and "horn down" position while doing figure 8s. Making the switch requires learning the intermediate spin to go from horn down to horn up, and the advanced spin to return to the horn down position. Such techniques are discussed in detail in Chapter13 (Cane Spinning).

Finally, some potential adversaries may at first seek to move around you, to see if you can maneuver in that position. You should be equally competent to move in a circular pattern with no trouble. Just be sure there are no walls or hindrances when turning.

What the Assailant Sees

Chapter Seven

Pressure Points

Pressure points are positions on the body where a minimal strike can cause significant pain, maybe disorientation, and sometimes crippling effects. While different martial arts schools vary as to the number of pressure points on the body, for cane fighting there are only nine that I feel you need to know.

Don't confuse martial-arts pressure points with the hundreds of healing medical pressure points in Chinese medicine. There is only a small overlap between the two systems.

Cane's Effect on Pressure Points

Magnified Power

> With a cane, depending on how you strike, your jab or blow may be magnified many times, producing enough power to break bones.

Unknown Medical Effect

> To understand the effect of a stick hitting these vital points, you will need to discuss such consequences with a medical doctor. Not being a physician, I

am NOT a reliable source on the medical aspects of these strikes. Further, I am only highlighting critical parts of what I think may be helpful in a self-defense situation.

Pressure Points on Front of Body

I am only discussing pressure points on the front of the body. Unless you are an advanced student, sidestepping to the back of an attacking person requires considerable skill and practice. Besides, strikes to the back side of the body (such as the kidneys, the base of the neck, and other vital points) are probably no more damaging than those to pressure points on the front of the body.

The Head

Big Pressure Point

The head should be a cane pressure point, but not its separate parts. What about the temple, just below the nose, the jaw hinge, and other painful parts of the head? You don't have the time or skill to aim that carefully unless you are an advanced cane student. The odds of hitting one of these specific points with a stick in the heat of battle are very small. Besides, the cane is a blunt striking instrument that will damage anyone when striking hard at his head. Use the whole head as your target.

Types of Injuries

Doctors see head injuries from falls, impacts during contact sports, people slipping off ladders, and garden-variety falls. They even encounter injuries from people standing up and hitting their heads on low ceilings. Because these types of injuries are common, doctors have a reasonably good idea of the varieties of damage done when a blunt object hits the head.

The most common results of such head injuries are a concussion, internal bleeding, or a cracked skull, any of which could lead to temporary or permanent memory issues. In certain situations, a powerful strike could ultimately result in death. It would take a doctor to describe all the possible outcomes. In summary, you can do such severe damage that it's not worth the risk, unless your life is in real danger.

Injuries to the head are hard to predict. So much depends on the speed and direction of the impact and the health of the victim. My eighty-one-year-old father-in-law fainted, fell on a carpeted floor, and suffered severe intracranial bleeding similar to that of a massive stroke. Yet there was only a slight impact on his head.

Conversely, I once stood up and hit the top of my head on a cabinet. The pain was excruciating for a day, and the lump on my head took almost a month to recede, yet it did no real damage. It is tough to specify the extent of suffering from a significant head strike, but it will most likely stop the fight.

Police Instructor's Advice

According to Wikipedia, police instructor Arthur Lamb trained over 10,000 officers. Part of his standard speech on use the baton included the following:

"In every class, I ask the officers if they've ever seen a subject subdued with one blow to the head. None of them ever have. What you're doing when you hit a man in the head is first, creating a serious danger of death, and second, you're numbing the one part of the body that can stop him. ... If you hit him in the head and put him into a state of shock where he is almost immune to pain, and now enraged beyond reason, the only thing left for you to do is beat him into the ground. This is why so many police brutality charges came about when batons were used the old-fashioned way."

Author's Advice

With a cane you multiply the force of your strike, and beginners seldom know how hard they are hitting. Given the sensitivity of the head and brain, you should never hit someone's head unless you are fighting for your life. I urge you instead to concentrate on other pressure points.

Eyes

You could thrust the point of the cane into the eye, usually as a counter to a close-in attack. The pain of being poked in the eye is so disabling that it ends the fight. Of course, a jab could also ruin vision in the attacker's eye or even break the eyeball.

Additionally, Wikipedia discusses the neurologic effect of a strike to the eye. "The Oculocardiac reflex... [can cause] a decrease in pulse rate associated with... compression of the eyeball." This nerve travels to the heart and can even cause electrical abnormality, which could be "life-threatening." I do NOT support causing permanent damage if other options are available, because after the fight the opponent might sue you. A defense attorney's fear is the attacker will walk down the aisle of the courtroom with a big eye patch and "accidentally" bump into chairs. In my opinion, jurors are not receptive to nor understanding of defendants who have caused eye injuries. So I would use an eye shot only if you fear for your life.

The Neck

Side of Neck

A whack (sideways swing) on the side of the neck

can often drop the assailant to the ground. I suppose, with enough force, it could break his neck. The vagus nerve runs along the side of the neck; a sharp jolt to it can cause unconsciousness. You might also compress the carotid artery, which also lies on the side of the neck, disrupting the flow of blood to the brain. This is a highly effective pressure point but also a potentially dangerous one for your opponent. There is the risk of permanent injury, and this technique might have legal consequences. For this reason, I dislike any targets above the collarbone unless necessary in an emergency.

Below the Adam's Apple

The indentation in your throat just below the Adam's apple is known in anatomy as the suprasternal notch. It is a significant, easily visible depression or dip at the base of the throat, where the neck joins the sternum. (Se the picture on the next page.) Even a mild strike to the suprasternal notch produces a severely debilitating sensation. I believe if you crushed the trachea, you could even kill someone. Even a light poke or thrust to this spot with a cane tip will back up any attacker, and a stronger push could collapse the trachea or larynx and cause someone to choke.

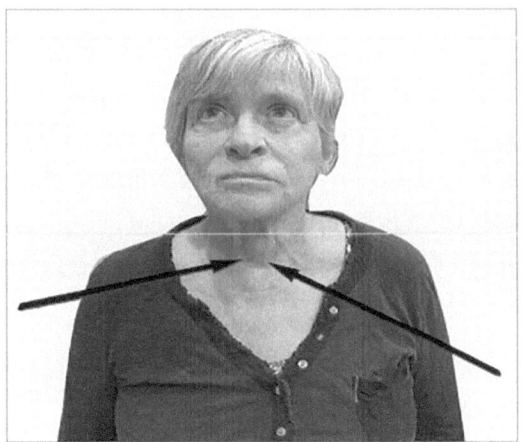

If someone is close to you or stepping close in a threatening manner, a cane tip in the suprasternal notch will back up anyone. For this reason, it is a commonly used vital point, but because of the potential damage, the push should be light.

The Sternum (Breastbone)

When many people hit the breastbone, they mistakenly believe they have struck the solar plexus, a nerve bundle in the middle of the body. Instead, they have smashed into the breastbone. A medium strike will bruise the sternum, causing pain and some difficulty breathing. A strong attack can break the breastbone, and possibly a rib or two, and can cause breathing difficulties. It also will either stop the fight or distract the attacker enough to land another strike. If the chest is compressed enough (which I believe is unusual from a trust of a cane tip), it could damage internal organs. The bottom of the breastbone is a small triangle that hangs down, medically called the xiphoid process. If this is broken, it could damage other organs.

The Armpit

The armpit is exposed whenever someone throws a strike, and a thrust of the cane tip under the arm causes pain and may, for a few seconds, make it difficult for the person to move his arm. This strike is especially helpful as a first strike against a boxer's left jab. Normally, when you strike under the arm, you immediately follow up with a second strike.

The Groin Area

The groin area is composed of two parts. The first is between the legs, and on a man, you're talking the penis and the scrotum. The second part (sometimes called the inguinal region) is the golden triangle between the waist and the top of your legs.

The Testicles

Every man fears getting hit in the balls. This small area is packed with sensitive nerves that are unprotected by any bone or muscle. An intense strike to this area will usually drop a man to the ground instantly as he rolls around in pain. Since the testicles produce sperm, a hard-enough attack could make a man infertile.

Golden Triangle

A strike to the golden triangle produces sharp, often debilitating pain, but it is nowhere near as strong as the pain caused by a strike to the testicles. Since the pubic bone is there, a strong hit could break that bone and rupture the bladder.

The Knees

The knees are highly susceptible to a lateral blow from a swing. The ligaments and tendons that provide knee stability are not designed for intense sideward pressure. A lateral strike will usually tear the ligaments, causing the person to fall. Don't waste your time hitting the knee cap straight on; you may damage it, but it will not be nearly as debilitating as a lateral strike.

The Arms and Legs

A cane blow (one-handed or baseball-type swing) anywhere on the arms or legs will cause excruciating pain and sometimes may temporarily deaden any feeling in that limb. If the strike is powerful enough, you can crack a bone or even completely break it. A blow to the shin bone is very painful, and a powerful strike will break that bone. The pain may even stop the fight.

Chapter Eight

Nature of Punching Attacks

The reason you carry a self-defense cane is so that if someone attacks, you are ready. That means you should assume anyone could attack you. When you first start your training, force yourself to mentally look over anyone approaching. Determine: If they were going to attack you, which hand would they use? After a week of consciously watching strangers approach, you will probably find you do so without thinking about it. But your body will almost automatically acknowledge how they approach. (The next chapter discusses how to defend yourself against punches.)

Right-Handed Punch

Most attacks start with a punch. If you have nothing to go on, then know that 90 percent of the world's population is right-handed. Therefore, you are generally safe in assuming the attack will start with a right-handed punch. (I had one instructor disagree, saying, "Wait for the first punch." In my opinion, that is like closing the barn door after the horse has escaped. You need those extra few seconds to be prepared for your opponent's attack. Some instructors say to look for which hand your opponent wears his watch on. That works only if he is wearing a watch, it is visible on his wrist, and you have time to notice.)

Roundhouse Right Blow

Few street-fighters have taken boxing or martial arts training. When they punch, statistically, they will begin by throwing a roundhouse punch. The only exception is noted below when the person squares up with the left hand forward.

Boxer's Left Jab

If the person is right-handed and has his left hand forward, he has probably had boxing training. He will probably throw one or a series of left jabs, which are fast punches with little power. He is trying to create an opening for a follow-up with a powerful right punch.

Philosophy of the Cane

If your attacker is going to punch you, he must be in striking distance. The striking space is generally two feet or less in front of you. You need only strike with a thrust of your cane tip to back him away. Alternatively, you can block the punch with the cane and swing in a counterattack at the leg, arm, or body.

Why Risk Your Life

This next piece of advice is a controversial and differs between instructors. Do whatever seems appropriate for you in the circumstances. For example, if someone approaches me armed with a knife or gun, I will give him whatever he wants.

At my peak, years ago, we practiced with a 22-gauge starter pistol that shot blanks. In the gym, I could disarm someone who stuck a gun in my face ten times out of ten. (Now, so many years later, when my speed is so much slower, I could probably neutralize the gunman only 20 percent of the time.) But even at my peak, I probably would have given the attacker my wallet. Money and credit cards can be replaced, but if something goes wrong, you are left dead or with a bullet hole.

Beware of Cocking the Fist

It is rare to find an untrained street fighter who will not cock his fist before striking. Sometimes they will step so they are forty-five to eighty degrees to you (almost perpendicular), so they can hide their movement while pretending they are scratching their ear, mustache, or upper lip.

According to what police friends tell me, when an attacker puts his hand near his face, he is usually covertly cocking his fist. Anytime you see that behavior, be prepared. As stated, a punch is especially likely if he has his foot back for better support.

Additionally, if you see someone's hand, usually their right hand, behind their back at belt level while they look belligerently at you, assume an on-guard position. This person may be reaching for a gun or a knife behind his back or in his belt.

If you are wrong, and are in the on-guard position but have not initiated an attack, it is, as they say, "no harm, no foul." You are ready for an attack that may not materialize, but if it does happen, you have a better chance of prevailing.

Arm cocked, ready to throw punch, disguised as ear scratch.

On-Guard Stance

If you see the person beginning to pull back his fist, don't wait. Immediately assume your on-guard position, and if you have time, strike first. In my opinion, you will be defending yourself from an imminent attack.

Roundhouse and Straight Punch

Of the dozen or so different punches that exist, statistically, ninety-seven percent (97%) of the strikes you might face are either straight punches or roundhouses. As a reminder, as earlier mentioned, if a right-handed man throws straight left jabs at you, he has probably had training in boxing or karate. I may be naive, but I like to think trained fighters usually do not prey on men with a cane.

Straight Punch

A straight punch is as described. It comes from the body in a straight line. It is a punch that takes practice to perfect and is seldom employed by an untrained assailant. Notice there is almost no difference at the beginning, middle and end of the punch in the distance between the elbow and your body. The punch ends almost perpendicular to the body and in a straight line.

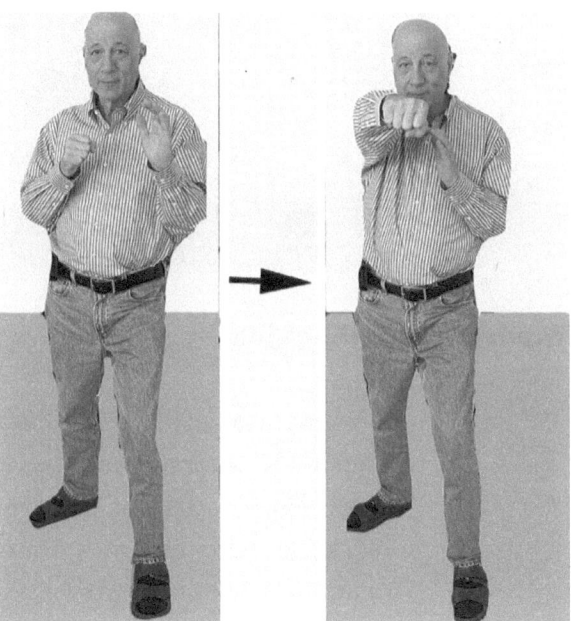

Roundhouse Punch

A roundhouse punch goes by various names. In karate, it is known as "mawashi-tsuki," but on the street, it is commonly called a roundhouse or haymaker punch. The blow travels in a somewhat squashed semicircular fashion. Often an assailant using such a punch will throw his shoulder into the strike to make it more powerful. The knuckles of the fist are often turned almost vertically. Usually, the punch is aimed at the jaw or the side of the body. Notice in the middle of the punch how far away the elbow is from the shoulder.

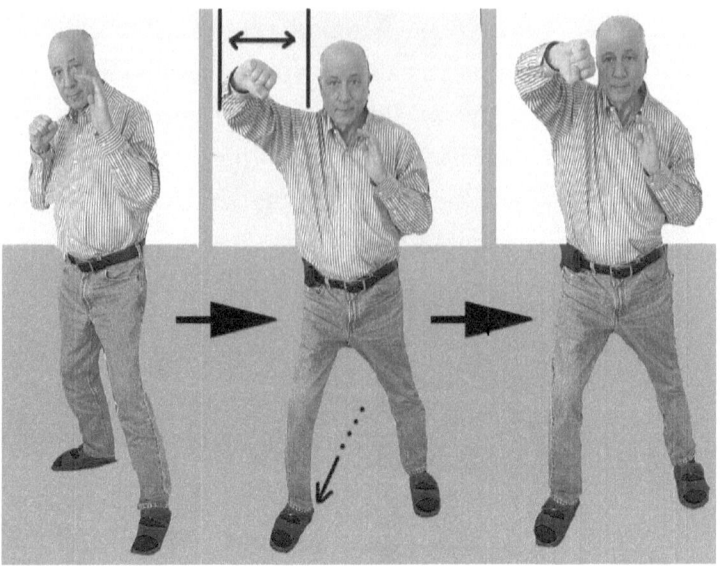

Importance in Blocking

The importance of the difference between a straight punch and a roundhouse lies mostly how you block them. With a straight jab, you can either parry or block the strike. However, since a roundhouse travels in an arc, unless you are trained, you should only try to block it. It can be parried, but this requires stepping safely to the outside as you move your cane. That additional step takes practice and concentration. Stick to the block; it is just as effective and easier.

Bock Only Forearm

To block a punch, you strike the forearm between the elbow and the wrist. You block a punch here because of the biomechanics of structural kinesiology, which is a fancy way of saying it takes far less energy. As I tell my students, hold out your arm as in a punch. Now have someone try to move your arm by pushing against your upper arm near the shoulder. It takes a great deal of energy to move your arm because your pectoral muscles contract and hold your upper arm in a strong position. Now have that same person take one finger and push against your wrist right at the joint. Your hand will move easily, as nothing is holding it in place.

So it takes very little energy to block a punch by hitting the forearm. It also takes far less time to block a punch as it reaches you than to reach out and stop it midstream. And blocking the forearm as the punch reaches you also means you have a smaller amount of territory to protect, because you know the punch is probably aimed at your head or upper body.

The Basic Law

This is not a book about law, but the law applies every time you use the cane. As I said earlier, I published a book on the subject,[1] and I assume there are also many other books that discuss the law of self-defense. You would be well advised to read one of these books or do research on the web. Remember, you could risk both criminal investigation and potential civil lawsuits, regardless of the situation. Know your rights ahead of time, and what to say to the police, should they be called to investigate.

Muscle Memory

The next section of this chapter discusses the effects of the "fight-or-flight" response (and your body's release of norepinephrine) on your ability to calmly and effectively use the techniques you are leaning. Your goal is to practice these techniques until they burn into your "muscle memory." You should be able to do them almost without thinking. It is the quick, almost automatic response that makes the techniques so very effective.

Fn. 1 Defend Yourself with Ju-Jitsu or Karate and Stay Out of Jail: Using Criminal and Civil Laws of Self-Defense to Your Advantage. (Through Amazon.com)

While others may disagree, I feel you only need to memorize about a dozen techniques. Yes, more would help give you a broader background, but in an emergency, you only need to respond in a few ways to be effective.

Visualization

After you have worked a particular technique into muscle memory, it is beneficial to practice it, even if for a short time, a little each month to keep it fresh in your memory.

Another technique that can augment and improve your techniques is visualization. Visualization is imagining yourself performing the selective technique step-by-step in your memory and performing it perfectly and accurately perfect at each stage of action. Professional athletes often use visualization to sharpen their skills.

Visualization has another use as well. There were several years when, for health reasons, I was unable to practice my martial arts. Every so often, I would diligently visualize myself running through all the techniques I have learned. I found over the years that when I was able to return to the martial arts, I found that my speed and executing the moves had decreased. However, most of the techniques were still fresh in my mind, and I could perform them correctly. I credit retention of my ability in significant part to visualization. Close your eyes and see an attacking throwing a punch, and you correctly moving your body and cane to block that punch and deliver a counterstrike. When you can't practice as much as you would like, I urge you to consider mental role-playing.

Breathing Countering Adrenalin Rush

Fight-Flight Response

When you are scared, your body automatically drops into the "fight-or-flight" response pattern. The fight-or-flight response affects all animals, including humans, when they are faced with danger. The body is bathed in hormones and undergoes physiological reactions in preparation to either fight or flee from the threat. Without getting overly technical, the adrenal glands secrete epinephrine, which causes the release of the hormone cortisol, while neurotransmitters release dopamine and serotonin. There are other hormones involved as well in this complex cycle.

As a result of the hormone bath, you immediately become "fight-or-flight" ready. Your blood pressure increases significantly, and your body releases sugar, giving you a burst of energy. You cannot process minute detail, only broad facts. Digestion slows down as all energy is transferred to your large voluntary muscles, which are necessary to fight or flee from the danger. Your vision changes to tunnel vision, which causes loss of your peripheral vision. Often you begin shaking. There is a reduction in fine motor skills, making activities like trying to bend someone's fingers difficult. All power is shifted to gross motor muscles, allowing you to punch harder and run faster.

Effect on Fighting Ability

When you are relaxed and practicing the techniques, you can think calmly and in detail. By analogy, think of yourself walking on a treadmill. But when you are actually being attacked, you do not always have the luxury of thinking clearly. As your hormones bathe you, by analogy, it is like running full speed on a treadmill.

I remember an incident that happened many years ago in San Francisco. One of my students, who had been with the school for about two years, was attacked on the street near her home. We always taught moves in a sequence of three strikes, so that if the first strike did not disable the attacker, you automatically moved on to your second move without having to think about what to do next.

The girl later told me, with some obvious embarrassment, that she did the first move, and the assailant dropped to the ground in pain. However, she was so high on adrenaline that she yelled to the attacker: "Get up, get up! I have two more moves." Then, as the adrenaline bath diminished, the girl reddened and realized how foolish this sounded. When you are high on hormones, you do not always think or act clearly.

Repetition and Breathing

This is why you practice these moves over and over, at least a hundred times a day, so they become embedded in "muscle memory." Your forebrain does not ve to think about how to react. Instead, it sets in motion a prearranged sequence of moves already drilled into memory. One way to reduce the effect of the fight-or-flight hormonal bath is to breathe deeply and regularly. By controlling your breathing, you lessen the impact of the adrenaline and other hormones temporarily controlling your body.

One well used method, often called combat breathing, or numerous other terminology, has you breathe in through your nose for three seconds. Then hold your breath for three seconds. Now breath out though your mouth for the same three seconds. Finally, hold your breath for three seconds, then repeat the cycle.

Chapter Nine

Defense to Punches

You know from the last chapter the main types of punches. You learned which to block or parry and how to breathe; you are now ready for actual self-defense against such strikes. I purposely am not demonstrating any attacks above the collarbone (the neck and head), as they can do serious injury and should be used only if you are in fear of serious injury or for your life.

I am also presenting only a few defense techniques to a punch. When you learn from a book, it is better to perfect a few effective techniques than to be overwhelmed with too many. Drill these into your muscle memory, and they will serve you well.

Roundhouse Right, Blocked

Step Back as Block

It sounds impossible that something as simple as stepping back will prevent you from being punched. But the length of the average person's arm, and thus the range of his punch, is only two feet to two feet four inches. When you are standing two feet away, your opponent feels he has a reasonable chance of hitting you. But if you step back about twelve inches, even if you miss the block, the punch will still stop short of catching you. You must step back as you block the strike. If you step back too soon, your attacker will just step forward before striking. Notice the distance in the picture below.

Use in the Streets

Nearly all untrained fighters on the street will try to hit you with a roundhouse punch. (See chapter 8 if you are unsure what a roundhouse strike is.)

Striking Block to Arm, Strike to Leg, Strike to Ribs

1. **Step**. Because you have the luxury of an extra three-foot extension to your reach, you can easily step back and remain in striking position.

2. **Block by Striking Arm**. As you step back for safety, raise your cane for a one-handed inside block. As always, strike (block) on the forearm. It is not easy to tell from the angle of this picture, but I am inside

and within the width of my opponent's shoulders. If your cane tip is elsewhere, use one hand to wave it in an overhead arc and bring it down on your assailant's forearm.

3. **Strike the Middle of the Leg**. Usually you would strike the leg closest to you with a one-handed strike. However, as this picture shows, you can, if warranted, instead hit the outside leg. You may have to reach, but it is possible.

4. **Cock the Cane**. Before delivering a powerful strike, it is often advantageous to either cock the cane (as in this picture) or swing it in a wide arc to generate speed and power for your strike.

5. **Horizontal Rib Strike.** Take a full, round swing across your attacker's body horizontally to his exposed ribs. If for some reason his arm is in the way, then

strike the arm instead, but usually the ribs are open. Strike the bottom ribs (the last two floating ribs) if you can aim your strike.

6. **Groin Strike**. If the assailant is still standing and looking threatening, follow up with a two-handed jab to the groin. You could, of course, have made this strike a one-handed groin strike from the ground up. However, the two-handed nature of this strike demonstrates that you can mix-and-match strikes.

From Bayonet On-Guard Position to a Double Thrust Defense

1. **Step Back**. Step back with your right foot. Your opponent is aiming for where you were, not where your head is now, twelve inches farther back.

2. **Rising Block**. TKeep your two hands on the cane. Thrust upward, with the cane roughly parallel to the ground, to just below the top of your head. If the punch is anywhere between your solar plexus and the top of head, your rising block will sweep it up and over your head, preventing any damage.

3. **Groin Thrust.** After the punch is neutralized, quickly cock the cane with your right hand back by your hip. Now swiftly and forcefully thrust it into your attacker's groin.

4. **Solar Plexus Thrust.** If your opponent is still standing and threatening you, re-cock the cane back by your hip and forcefully thrust it into his solar plexus.

5. **Leg Strike.** In the unlikely event that your attacker is still standing and threatening you, follow up with

a one-handed swing to the legs. Again, you can mix one-handed and two-handed strikes to fit your needs.

Roundhouse Right, Outside Block

1. **Outside Block the Punch**. Instead of stepping back with your right foot to avoid the punch, instead step forward sideways with your left foot. It advances at about a forty-five-degree angle. This will put you outside of his body, so even if you were to miss the block, you would be safe from the punch. You should know that stepping to the outside, while not difficult, does take more skill than a simple block.

2. **Strike Arm as Step**. As you step, swing the cane in an overhead arc and strike the attacker's forearm. This is similar to a block, except that you are outside of his body and striking the outside of his forearm.

3. **Strike Ribs.** Using two hands, jab the ribs with a two-handed strike. Alternatively, you could do a one-handed swing and strike the ribs. The ribs are an excellent target. From the outside, they are open and available for any strikes you want to try.

4. **Leg Strike**. When you strike the leg, be sure to take a full swing. The strike's speed generates the power and strength of the impact on the shin bone.

Right and Left Blow

1. **The Combination**. It is not uncommon for someone to throw a right-and-left-punch combination in a fight. They decided before they moved to throw a sequence, and the left will follow very quickly after the right. You need to always be aware that you can encounter a right-left grouping, which is why you must remain observant when blocking a punch. A

left roundhouse may follow the right blow. It easy to block if you are expecting the possibility that might exist.

2. **The Blocks**. As you block the right with an inside strike, you see the left coming. You move the cane like a windshield wiper, pivoting at the elbow. Just a quick swipe to the left, hitting his forearm, is all you need. While it would be nice to punish your attacker in the strike, your real goal is just to deflect and block the punches so that you remain unharmed.

3. **Jab and Swing**. The final two strikes are a two-handed jab to the solar plexus, immediately followed by a one-handed swing to the ribs.

Boxer's Left Jab

When someone squares up to you with the left side of their body facing you, statistically, there is a good chance they have had boxing lessons. Boxers usually lead with their left hand, throwing fast jabs that are designed to distract you. If you are hit with a left jab, it may sting a little, but it is not a powerful punch. Instead, the strike is designed to open you up for a strong and powerful right punch. So you have two tasks with a left jab. First, be sure to block the blow. Second, keep your opponent away using quick jabs with the cane so that he can't throw the right-handed follow-up.

1. **Outside Block**. When you block, take two precautions. First, step forty-five degrees forward. This will place you outside the path of the punch should you fail to block it. Your block should deflect the punch, if not also punish the attacker. And because you are outside your opponent's shoulders, he would have to turn his body to throw a right blow at you.

2. **Rib Jab**. As your assailant throws his punch, he opens up his rib cage. By using a two-handed jab to the ribs, you hurt him and keep him farther away than he can punch. The extra two feet of the cane gives you this luxury. If your opponent is throwing multiple jabs before you make your next move, keep striking him in the ribs each time he hits.

3. **Swing to Back.** When you strike the back, you need to decide if you want the upper back or the lower back. The risk in hitting the lower back is that you rupture a kidney. The kidneys are about the size of a big fist, located just above the hip bone. Striking the upper back usually means bone pain or damage to the spinal cord.

Advanced Move

The following technique is included more for demonstration purposes than for self-defense. There are a wide variety of arm drag-downs, throws using the cane, and leg sweeps; some schools are quite excited about their inventive use. You need to know they exist, but why use them? They are fun for advanced students to play with in the studio, but I personally don't see any reason to employ them on the street. The cane is a tool best used for jabbing and swinging, not for hooking and trapping body parts. Still, so you will understand the concept, I am including one for show.

Leg Throw

1. **Step and Block.** For this technique, I am holding the cane at the other

end, so I will be striking and blocking with the crook end. As my opponent throws a roundhouse punch, I step back to give myself an extra twelve inches of security. Simultaneously, as I stride, I execute an inside block to my assailant's forearm.

2. **Catch Leg**. With the crook, I reach down and hook the assailant's leg. I catch the inside of his knee, although you can hook anywhere on the bottom part of the leg. I am doing a ju-jitsu type throw, which is different from a karate throw. You needn't worry about the difference, other than to note there are different ways of doing this throw.

3. **Pull and Step to Side.** As I pull the attacker's leg forward, I also step outside of his raised leg. In the photograph, you can see that the assailant has his left arm ready to punch. However, my assailant is unable to throw a left-handed strike with his leg raised and off balance, especially with my being to his side. My left arm is in the process of reaching for his shoulder.

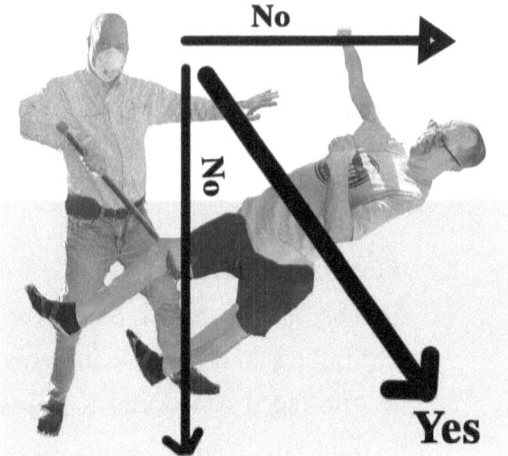

4. **Push at 45° Angle**. Because I am close to my assailant, I do not need to grab any clothing. I merely push him toward the ground at a forty-five-degree angle. If you drive his shoulder straight down or straight back, he will not fall to the ground.

5. **Final Notes**. While this is an effective throw, it is not a violent throw (except on those infrequent occasions when the opponent hits his head on the sidewalk and is dazed). For that reason, I usually recommend striking him on the leg or ribs with the cane before you do the throw. Remember, when you are standing and your opponent is on the ground, the law considers him to have withdrawn from combat. Any strikes you do will be as an aggressor and not in self-defense.

Preemptive Strikes

IIt is not uncommon for people with a cane, when confronted by a verbally aggressive individual, to consider making a preemptive strike. The strike could be a mild poke in the chest, indicating, "Don't mess with me." However, some people with a cane make a full-force offensive strike at an opponent's groin or Adam's apple. This is not a law book, but in general, you can defend yourself when you are in "reasonable fear" of "immediate attack" or "bodily injury" and you defend yourself with "reasonable force." As a rough general rule, initiating a preemptive strike is generally considered an unprovoked attack and is not recognized as justified self-defense.[1]

You will have to decide what actions are warranted and appropriate in the face of a verbal but belligerent individual confronting you

---

Fn. 1.   You would be well advised to know the basic principles of self-defense and what the law allows. Should you report an incident to the police, and if you do so, how do you frame your call to best protect yourself legally? What will the police ask, and how should you respond? Do you really need a lawyer?

Remember, when the police show up at a scene of a fight, they really don't know what happened, and you may be very surprised at the questions you are asked. If you don't reply appropriately, you might talk yourself into a jail cell even though you were only defending yourself. Also, your insurance policy might cover you in a civil lawsuit for the cost of an attorney. If you don't know all your rights, in my opinion, you are only half trained. If you want to know more about your rights, you can buy from Amazon.com my book Defend Yourself with Ju-Jitsu or Karate and Stay Out of Jail: Using Criminal and Civil Laws of Self-Defense to your Advantage.

You can also search the Internet for the laws on self-defense in your state. As another option, you could stop by your local public defender's office and talk to someone without charge. You can certainly ask a police officer, but I am not sure how knowledgeable they are on the nuances of self-defense. A Google search may reveal other books like mine written for the average person.

Chapter Ten

Defense to Kicks

Not Many Kicks

I've never been in a street fight, but many of our school's students have been involved in incidents over the years, and I've learned from them a considerable amount about street fights. It is infrequent in street fights against untrained fighters to find someone kicking you while you are upright. There are several reasons.

1. **Takes too much training**. Anyone can throw a punch, even if they don't do it correctly. The hands and arms are fast and, if used appropriately, damaging above the waist. But to kick forcefully takes considerable skill. An unskilled kicker risks being off balance. Without training, they can't execute proper kicks (i.e., karate or ju-jitsu kicks). So why kick when they are untrained in it, the adrenaline is flowing, and pressure is intense? You see kicks often on television but infrequently in the streets.

2. **Too close of range**. Many street fights happen in close quarters, the adversaries often within two feet of each other (the approximate length of an average man's arm). It is difficult to kick at that distance (except for knee kicks, which

few untrained fighters have mastered). Kicks are usually done by trained ju-jitsu and karate practitioners at a proper kicking distance, which is longer than two feet.

3. **Pants too tight.** People who train for kicks do so in loose trousers or karate-type uniforms. Tight jeans make kicks difficult and high kicks to the breastbone (sternum) or the head almost impossible.

4. **Off-balance and telegraphing**. Untrained fighters are often afraid of being off balance when they kick and even more fearful of the recipient grabbing their leg and throwing them to the ground. Also, many untrained individuals know that they telegraph their kicks, making capture even more likely.

When Kicks Are Used

You will rarely encounter a kicking attack while standing upright. It's not that it can't happen, but I've heard of kicks being used in street fights only in the two situations below.

1. Victim on the ground. The victim is lying flat on the ground, unmoving, and the opponent stomp-kicks him.

2. Victim getting up from ground. The victim is getting up from the ground, and while he is still on his knees, the attacker steps close and front-kicks him in the head or ribs. (When the victim falls back to the ground, the attacker may keep kicking.)

Marine and Special Training

It've spoken to marines and special forces personnel because I was anxious to know what unarmed self-defense they are being taught these days. The responses were unanimous: Except for a few moves, they are not trained to fight without weapons. They use their rifles, pistols, knives, or other tools in their possession. They don't expect to be unarmed in today's combat.

Marines are taught to kick in the two situations described above (when the opponent is lying helplessly on the ground or is getting up from the ground). Some training camps, but not many, teach kicking the opponent below the knee to distract him. The idea of one soldier throwing numerous kicks at another is a Hollywood fantasy.

In short, kicks are usually for trained martial artists fighting in cages or matches governed by rules and against other trained fighters. Competition fighting is a specialized sport, often involving many kicks performed by highly trained martial artists. The public sees theses professionals and erroneously assumes kicks are common.

Location of Kicks

If an untrained fighter is going to kick someone who is standing, it will almost always be to the groin, knees, or shins. It takes too much balance to kick above the waist, so don't expect any kicks to the solar plexus (breastbone) or head area.

Type of Kicks

Karate and some ju-jitsu schools primarily use three types of kicks: front kicks ("mae geri"), side kicks ("yoko geri"), and roundhouse kicks ("mawashi geri"). I included the Japanese names for the kicks should wish to Google the nature of those movements. Martial artists at higher levels train in many other kicks, including flying kicks, rear thrusts, and knee kicks. For street fighting, if you face a kick from an untrained fighter, it will almost always be a front kick.

Layman's Front Kick

There is a difference between a layman's front kick and a martial artist's front kick. A street fighter kicks typically with the hip as the fulcrum. The leg remains relatively straight.

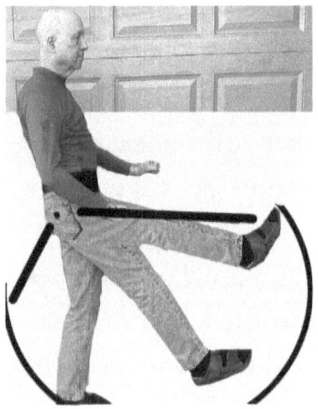

Conversely, a martial artist's front kick uses the knee as the fulcrum. The trained fighter raises his knee and then snaps the kick from the bent knee.

Blocking A Front Kick

Regardless of which type of front kick is delivered, the method for blocking it is the same. For the same reason you step back when your opponent throws a punch, you step back when blocking a kick. By taking a step back, you gain an extra twelve inches of safety should you fail to block the kick.

Defense #1

The first block is a two-handed downward cane block. Note that on this block I step back about twelve inches, giving myself a safety margin. The attacker kicks to where I was, not where I end up. The two-handed download block is a strong defense that should stop any forward kick. A common mistake among beginners is that they bend their back almost parallel to the ground to make the block. In this position, you cannot move quickly or see if any unusual activity is happening. It also weakens your block's strength. My eyes remain on the opponent during my entire my block.

Even if fail the block, kick misses by 12 inches

The cane gives you an extra three-foot advantage. Although I could take a small half step to bring me closer to my attacker, I am still able to reach him from my defensive stance. My back remains perfectly straight, and I am not sacrificing my ramrod-straight back to reach the assailant with the swing of my cane.

Because the attack was a kick, I prefer to deliver a punishing defensive move to one of his legs. There is, of course, great flexibility on which targets you choose.

The final strike is a two-handed jab to the solar plexus. Throughout this and the previous strike, I have not moved my feet. If you have stepped back too far, you can take a half step forward to bring you closer to your opponent.

Defense #2

In this defense, you make a powerful overhand swing to the leg, and this strike acts as a block, immediately stopping the kick. This technique is more advanced and requires slightly higher skill than an inside block does. With my left foot, I am stepping forward about twelve inches, but at a forty-five-degree angle. If you look closely, you can see that I am twelve inches away from my opponent's kick.

Even if I missed the block, his attack would not reach me. As before, my back is straight, so that I can move to the next position without having to straighten up and regain my balance.

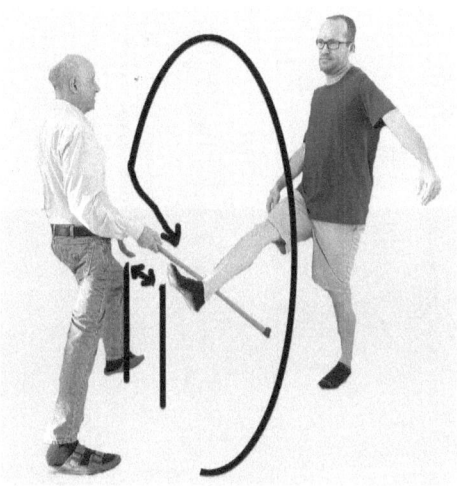

The second movement is an overhand swing to the opponent's leg. Note that I have not moved my stance and that my back remains straight. Some schools teach taking a half step before you strike, so that you will hit the opponent with the "sweet spot" of the cane (about eight inches from the tip). There is nothing wrong with taking a small step, but it costs you two to four seconds. I prefer the extra speed, but it is your choice.

The last swing is an overhead strike to the opponent's right arm. Students sometimes ask why I strike across the body. The answer is simple: My assailant kicked with his right leg, confirming that he was right-handed. Since his kick failed so miserably, he would most likely continue with a right punch if he wanted to strike again. Hopefully, my strike disables him or convinces him not to continue the attack. As always, my back remains straight, and I have not moved my feet.

Defense #3

This technique is almost the same as the outside block, but it takes less skill. You either keep your stance or, as I do, with your right foot step to the right, so that the kick will miss you even if you fail to block it. The follow-up moves are the same as for the outside block defense

Chapter Eleven

Defense Against Holds

- A. Front Choke
- B. Rear Bear Hug
- C. Front Bear Hug
- D. Rear Hand Choke
- E. Lapel Grips
- F. Wrist Grips

As I teach you to escape attacks, I am starting my discussion of each one with an unarmed escape technique. Why would a book on cane defense teach an unarmed technique? Because I have found over the years that when a person understands how easy it is to escape, and that it can be done even unarmed, they relax more. When the move is initiated, they don't panic. They learn the cane defense releases much faster, because they are remaining calm.

The second reason for including an unarmed move is to help you realize that although cane is effective, in an emergency, you can function without it. The cane is only one tool, albeit the most significant tool in your arsenal, but not your only option.

Remember that the cane gives you an extra three feet of reach, as well as a multiplier effect enabling you to strike with bone-breaking force.

A. Front Choke

Attack

The front choke happens when someone stands in front of you, usually with his arms locked straight, and places both his hands around your throat. His thumbs press into your Adam's apple or neck, choking you. If you analyze the attack, however, you realize all that is locking you is his fingers on the back of your neck. That is a fragile, precarious hold that can be easily broken. Such an attack is serious and would not warrant a simple pain-free escape on the street. However, understanding the getaway helps you know how weak the attack is, and how unconcerned you need to be for your life.

Limitations of Attack

You must practice the two unarmed escapes below, because only when you comprehend the weakness of the attack can you react calmly. Most people panic when their airflow is constricted. To remain calm, you must feel confident you can escape.

All you need to do is walk backward, and you can't be choked. Of course, you couldn't do this in a street fight, because the attacker would switch to another attack. But try it with a friend. Walking backward prevents the attacker from applying enough pressure to choke you effectively.

Unarmed Escape

A better pain-free break is to step back with your

right foot, but instead of dropping straight back, swing your right foot ninety degrees to your right. Your feet should now be parallel to each other, toes facing the same way, and you are effectively at ninety-degree angle to your attacker. As you step back, bring your left hand up and push his hands off your neck. You are now entirely free of the choke.

Remember, since a choke is a severe attack, in real life you would not risk a simple pain-free escape. Instead, you would follow up with punishing strikes or a devastating ju-jitsu lock or throw.

Cane Escape #1

Step back to relieve the choking pressure, and swing the cane up between his legs. Then swing laterally to strike his ribs.

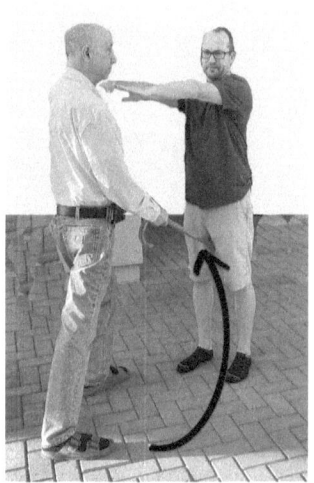

Cane Escape #2

Step sideways, so you are outside of his shoulders, as you bring the cane up and around, swatting off his hands around your neck. Be sure to hit his forearms, preferably near his wrists rather than his upper arms. As you strike, you will find his right side wide open. Take a one-handed swing at his ribs, then up between his legs.

B. Rear Bear Hug

Attack

Your assailant comes up behind you and puts his arms around you, usually grabbing his other wrist or hand to make a secure locking mechanism. He then tries to squeeze and hurt you. There are two different types of rear bear hug attacks. In the first, his arms are around you but your arms are free. In the second, he has his arms wrapped around your arms, so that your arms are pinned to your body as he encircles you from the rear.

Limitations of Attack

Because your assailant has both arms wrapped around you, he is in a static position. You have ample time to escape if you relax and have committed your escape to muscle memory. Obviously, if you have a cane, you will use it to protect yourself. The sole purpose of understanding the unarmed version is to realize you do not need to panic.

Unarmed Escape

The first part of the defense is to swivel your hips to the side so that you have a clean shot at his groin. Since his grip is above your waist, moving your hips is not difficult. Then swing your arm down hard with the edge of your hand ("judo chop"), striking hard into his groin. Do it twice if he does not release you the first time. Naturally, since you are under a serious attack, you would follow up with additional strikes.

Cane Escape #1

A rear bear hug is easy to escape when you have a cane. Take the crook of the cane and fit it between your body and your opponent's clasped hands. Now pull down, breaking the hold. The opponent is unable to retain his grip under the downward pressure of the cane. At the same time, step forward and turn to the side. With both hands on the cane, strike backward into your assailant's solar plexus. If he is still threatening you, follow up with a two-handed jab to his groin.

Cane Escape #2

If the opponent grabs you under the arms, your arms are free, and your escape is easy. Just take the cane and swing it down at his legs behind you. Alternatively, as in the unarmed escape, you can just pivot your hips to the side and strike the cane between his legs. If you want, you can reverse the cane grip and pull the crook up into his crotch, lifting him onto his toes.

C. Front Bear Hug

Attack

Your assailant comes up to you, face to face, and puts his arms around you, usually grabbing his other wrist or hand in a seemingly secure grip. As with the rear bear hug, there are two different types of attacks. In the first front bear hug attack, his arms are around you, but your arms are free. In the second, he has his arms wrapped around your arms as he encircles your body.

Unarmed Escapes

If your arms are not free, it seems at first glance as if your attacker has you immobilized. The first part of the escape is to drive your two thumbs into his groin. Take your thumbs and aim for his penis. It may sound obnoxious, but it is a very effective move. Your opponent will back up, as shown in the picture.

Now grab his waist with both hands. He is still leaning on you, so your balance is somewhat compromised, and holding on to your attacker gives you more stability. After the thumbs to the groin, he is far enough away that your kick will not be smothered. Bring your knee up sharply into his groin. Do it twice. After the knee kicks, he should drop his hands from you. If he doesn't, swing your elbow across his chin. Do not hit his chin straight on; instead, hit the side of his cheek and spin his head.

Cane Escape

The first thing you do to escape from a front bear hug

is to pivot your hips so you have a direct shot at the aggressor's groin. Swing your cane up between his legs. At the same time, step back with your right foot. Strike between his legs to loosen his hands and make it easy to step back. Then, using a two-handed grip, thrust the cane into the assailant's solar plexus.

 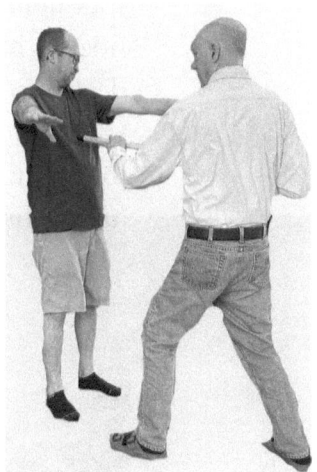

D. Rear Hand Choke

Attack

The attack is similar to the front choke, except the attacker chokes you from behind. He puts both hands around your neck, arms usually straight, and squeezes your windpipe, choking you. When you analyze the attack, you realize all that is holding you is his fingers on the front of your neck—a fragile hold that can be easily broken.

Unarmed Escape

Assuming you are right-handed, reach up with your

right arm. Keep it close to your body, and don't move your shoulder. You don't want to telegraph your move. Now grab his right hand, which is gripping your neck. Twist your palm inward so that your thumb goes against the back of his hand and your four fingers grab his palm. If that is hard to do, then wait until you start your turn to get your fingers inside his hand. Now swing your left foot around 180 degrees so that you are facing him. Continue to twist your hand as your turn. Now put your left hand on top of his left hand. Then, with both hands, twist (throw) him to the ground.

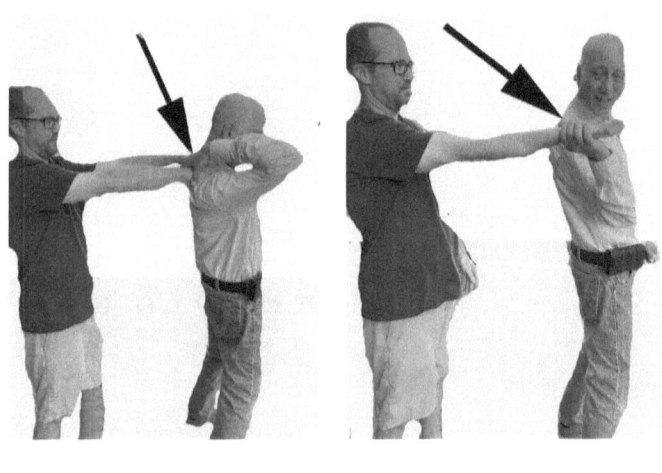

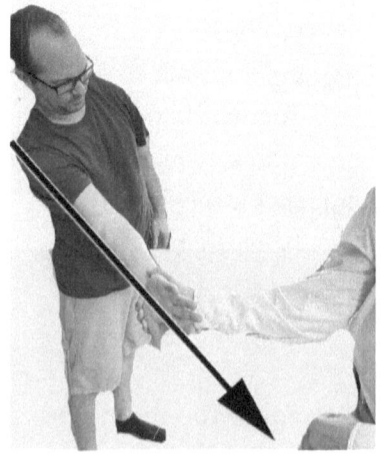

Cane Escape #1

When your opponent is choking you from the rear, as mentioned earlier, all he has holding you are the tips of his fingers. Step forward with your left foot and then swing around to your left 180 degrees. You are now facing your assailant. At the same time, swing the cane in a circle, hitting his forearms (preferably near his wrists). The action will rather violently dislodge the attacker's arms from your neck. From this position, swing and strike his lower leg. If the aggressor still seems like he wants to continue the attack, make a two-handed jab at his solar plexus.

Cane Escape #2

Leave your cane facing tip down. Step forward with your left foot and pivot 180 degrees so that you are facing your opponent. Now bring your cane swiftly up between his legs. Then quickly make a two-handed jab to his solar plexus.

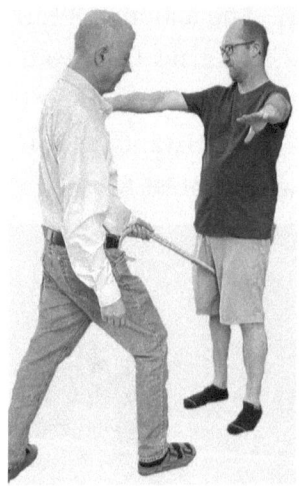 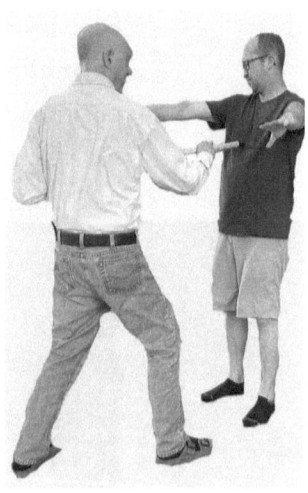

E. Lapel Grip

Attack

In a lapel grip, the attacker grabs either your shirt or your jacket with one hand or two hands. If the person's attack involves only a one-handed grip, watch his other hand to make sure it is not cocked to punch. If he does try to punch, then first block that punch (as described in chapter 4), before you dislodge his grip. If the aggressor has both hands on your clothes, it is much easier to defend yourself. Both hands are visible and locked in position, so you know he is not going anywhere.

Cane Escape

The defense to a lapel hold is similar to many other techniques when the attacker's hands are stretched out. You swing the cane between his legs and then strike in the solar plexus. When preparing for the groin swing, be sure you do not telegraph the strike by looking down or smiling. Don't move your shoulders; the attack originates and pivots from the elbow.

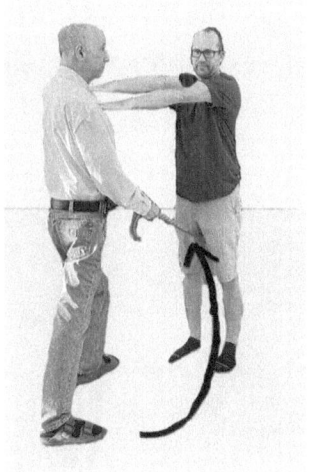 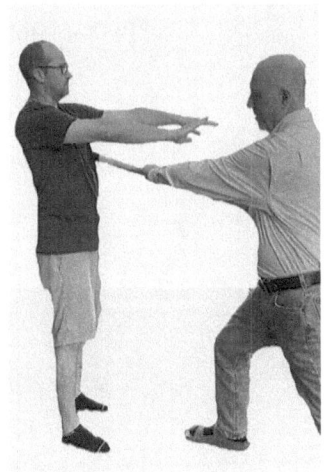

F. Wrist Grips

Occasionally, someone may grab your wrist, usually the arm holding the cane. (If he instead grips the cane, your escape options are covered in the next chapter.) When your assailant grabs your wrist, you must decide if you want to punish him. If it does not seem a severe attack, you may just want to free yourself without causing him pain.

Defense #1

This first wrist escape is so simple it often amazes beginners, who may have the notion that once the cane is in a specific hand, it must remain in that location. Nothing could be further from the truth. The reason you practice cane spinning is to become comfortable transferring the cane between hands. Assume the cane is in your right hand, and he grabs your right wrist. All you do is flip up the tip of the cane so that your other hand can grasp it. When both hands on the cane, you release your right hand, the one he still holds, and transfer the cane fully to your left hand. Now quickly swing it up between his legs. If your opponent looks aggressive, you may wish to first fake a head strike, before reverting to a groin swing.

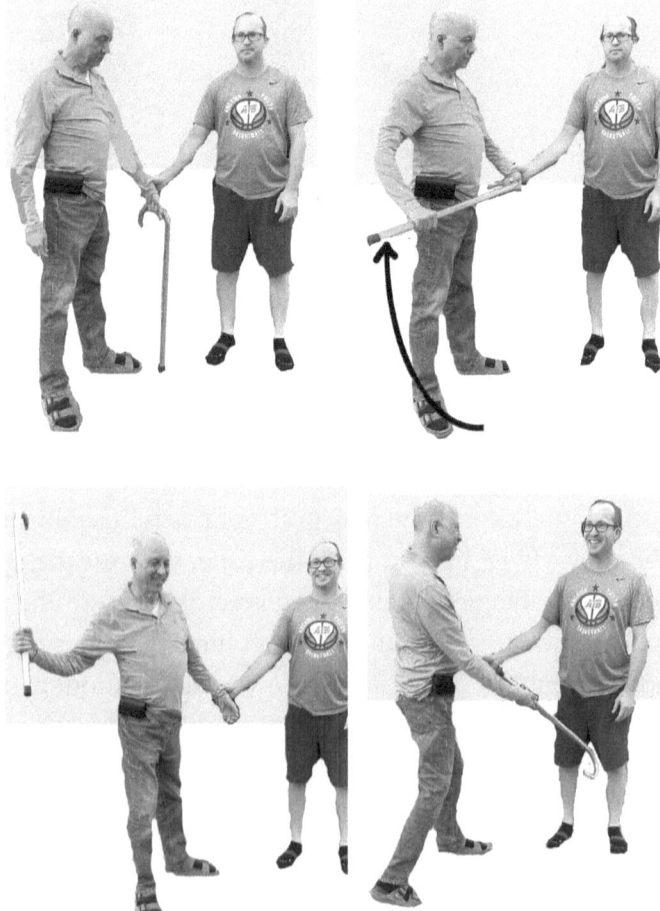

Defense #2

In the second technique, you are not trying to punish your assailant; instead, you just want him to release his hold. Again, assume he grabs your right wrist, which is holding the cane. Bring the tip up behind his arm without disturbing his grip. The tip is now facing the sky. Reach across your body with your left arm, and seize the cane above his hand.

Now step forward to his side as you twist the cane clockwise. Your attacker will have to let go of the cane or be dragged down to the ground.

Chapter Twelve

Cane Grabs

When you wave the cane around enough, it is eventually going to dawn on your opponent that you intend to use it as a threatening instrument. Many attackers will decide to take the cane away from you, either to stop your aggressive behavior or to capture the cane and use it against you.

Your attacker shouldn't be able to get close enough to secure a hold on your cane, but if he does, you need to know how to dislodge his grip. Your escape is, in large part, based on the principles of aikido. The three key components of aikido are harmonizing linear strength, redirecting attacks with a circular motion, and twisting joints in directions where they don't naturally go.

Aikido Principles

Harmonize Strength

The best way to understand harmonizing linear strength is to think of never resisting your opponent's strength. Assume you have five units of force, and your opponent has ten. If you get into a pushing contest, you will lose. Your attacker's ten units will quickly overwhelm your five units. He will push you to the ground.

Instead, when the assailant moves with his ten units of strength, you sidestep and pull with your five units. Now your fifteen units prevail over his mere ten. In summary, you never directly oppose his force but instead seek to combine it with your efforts to overcome him.

Redirect with Circular Motion

When your opponent attacks you with a punch, kick, or push, he is moving in a straight line. It would take considerable force to stop that movement with another linear force, such as a straight-line block. Instead of meeting his strike with power, you intercept it with a circular motion. You don't stop his linear motion (say, a punch) but instead turn his direct force against him as part of a circular motion.

You synchronize your movement with the speed of his attack. You release your opponent from the circular motion when it will do him the most harm to him. When he is ejected from the circular motion, his balance is broken, and he is severely disadvantaged.

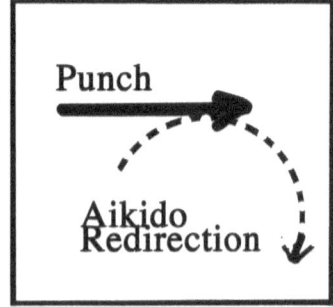

During these movements, you retain your balance. Indeed, your legs, hips, and back combine to provide the power to your circular motion. Don't bother trying to digest the textual explanation; things will become clear as you read the chapter.

Joint Control

Most joints in the body, such as the elbow, wrist, shoulder, and knee, are designed to flex in limited directions. In aikido, you capture a joint and twist it in an unnatural direction. You may, for example, twist a wrist, causing the elbow to turn, which in turn throws the shoulder joint into an awkward motion. To avoid breaking a joint, the opponent must voluntarily throw himself in that direction.

Pivot point ("fulcrum"). Here we need a brief review of high school physics. The pivot point ("fulcrum") is the fixed point on which the lever rests. Moving the pivot point either makes everything pivot more easily or causes it to take more strength.

>**Fulcrum in middle**. Remember the simple teeter-totter (see-saw) you used as a child. It is a long, narrow board resting on a pivot in the middle. When one end goes up, the other goes down. With the fulcrum in the middle, if one side has a child weighing fifty pounds, the other end needs a child of equal weight in order to go up while the other end goes down. .

>**Fulcrum near end**. If you move the pivot point closer to the fifty-pound child, then the lever is very long, and minimal effort (force) is needed to move the fifty-pound child up and down; a much lighter child could do it.

>**Application to arm**. You don't need any more physics, except to understand that if

the pivot point is the wrist, and you twist that wrist, the twisting motion can force the elbow and even the shoulder to also twist. If the fulcrum point is the elbow, then you can twist the joint about, the shoulder, when you twist or bend the elbow.

Summary

In executing the cane release techniques, you will find that these three principles of aikido are applied continuously. Because this is only an introduction to escaping cane grabs, most of the procedures use the first two principles. However, all three come into play at various stages of the art. Additionally, because the cane is, in reality, a stick and can be used to hit someone, you will also be using the principles of karate in some of your defenses.

The obvious question is what to do if, during your escape technique, the opponent re-grabs the cane. If you make a move fast enough, he should not be able to re-grip the cane. However, if he does, continue with the same or another cane escape. If you have to release him two or three times before striking him, that is acceptable.

Notes on Practicing

An assailant can grab a cane in so many different ways. Broken down to the lowest common detonator, they are all just a grip on a piece of wood. The four the most common escapes, shown in this chapter, will solve most of your problems. When you practice, have the other person grab and re-grasp the cane until you can easily and quickly dislodge his hand or hands easily. Have your practice opponent be inventive, and you will find the principles of escape apply to all situations. They may need a little adjustment, depending on how much the person is pulling and in which direction.

Cane Grips While Standing

Avoidance Escape

The first escape is so obvious that it surprises many people. If you see someone reaching for your cane, there is no reason to let him get near it. All you need to do is move the cane out of the way, across your body, so your opponent cannot grab it.

If the assailant appears aggressive in disturbing you or in trying to catch your cane, a sharp swing to the legs should discourage him. When you move the cane out of the way, it should automatically be in ready-to-swing mode.

Small Circle Escape

Aikido generally uses large circular motions to neutralize an attack. But in the 1960s Grandmaster Wall-Jay popularized (if not created) what he called small-circle ju-jitsu. This particular cane technique requires that your pivot point be your wrist. You don't need to use—nor do you want to telegraph your actions by using—your elbows or shoulders. This technique will work circling clockwise or counterclockwise. Here your opponent has grabbed the tip of your cane with both hands. Assuming you are right-handed, reach out and grab the middle of the cane with your left hand.

Using your wrist, make a small circle with your cane tip. When you reach the top of your arc, press straight down toward the ground; don't continue in a circular motion. As you pull down, step back with your right foot to make it harder for your attacker to re-grab the cane. The technique also gives you room to give your attacker a straight jab to the groin or solar plexus area.

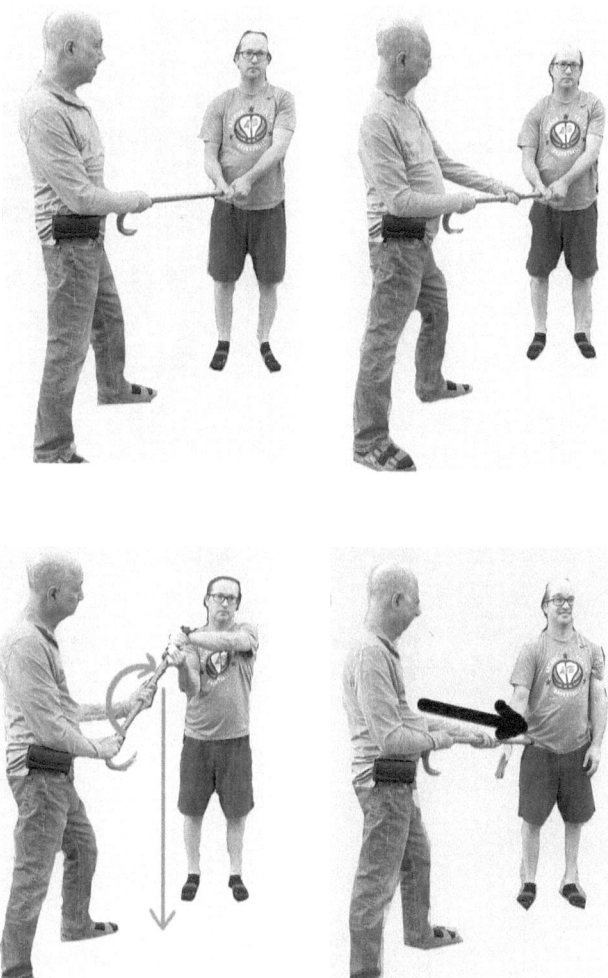

Large Circle Escape

Again your attacker has grabbed the tip of your cane with two hands. Grasp the middle of the cane's shaft with your other hand. Now swing the cane in a wide, counterclockwise circle. At the top of the arc, force the cane approximately straight down. Unlike the small-circle escape, this large circle will force the attacker's arms very low.

He is now wide open for an attack twisting him the ground or to a jam to the solar plexus. Since you have the added length of the cane, you should step back about a half step before striking.

You should also practice turning your circle clockwise. It will not be as effective, but it can still work. More important, it will help you appreciate the differences between the two ending positions. The more knowledge you have about how different circle directions affect the body, the better prepared you will be. Large-circle escapes differ greatly depending on the direction of the circle.

Middle Grip Escape

In this version, the attacker has grabbed the middle of your cane with two hands. If you haven't already, you should immediately grasp the cane's other end with your remaining hand. Your attacker's hands are between your holds.

Remember the basic principle of aikido: Do not directly oppose your attacker's force. The last thing you want to do is to get in a pushing or shoving match over possession of your cane. Quickly pivot on the toes of your left foot while raising the horn of the cane. Because you are moving in a circular direction and using your whole body, your opponent cannot resist.

As you turn the cane, take a full step with your left foot so that you have the power of your core body, adding to the pivoting of the stick. Keep turning so that you are now facing in the opposite direction. Both feet are planted on the ground, and your back is straight. If your attacker is still holding on, give him a push with your rear end to back him up a half step. Now pull the cane down with both hands to your waist level.

At the same time, pivot half a step to your rear, so you are perpendicular to the assailant. You are now in a position to strike his solar plexus, groin area, or his legs.him up at a half step. Now, pull the cane down with both hands to your waist level.

At the same time, pivot half a step to your rear, so you are perpendicular to the assailant. You are now in a position to strike his solar plexus, groin area, or his legs.

Cane Grips in a Wheelchair

The philosophy of cane escapes is equally applicable to people in wheelchairs. Move the stick in large circles, and don't oppose his force, but augment it in the opposite direction. Hold the cane in one hand, and if the opponent grabs it in one or two hands, grab it at both ends. Then move the cane in a circular motion in the opposite direction from the way the assailant is pulling; if he pulls to the right, move in a circular motion to the left, and vice versa. If he re-grabs your cane, it is just as easy to escape. Just keep repeating the escapes until you have full and compete possession of the cane. Sadly, you may need to use these techniques as you wheel along.

The best way to practice is to have your practice partner grab the cane, and you swing circularly and lean. First swing and lean to the right and then on the next grab to the left, but never opposing his strength. One way results in his letting go, the other way in a potential arm lock. It will help if you repeat these exercises at least five hundred times, so that they become second nature.

One difference between an escape standing and an escape sitting is that when sitting you may need to use a two-handed swing to the head.

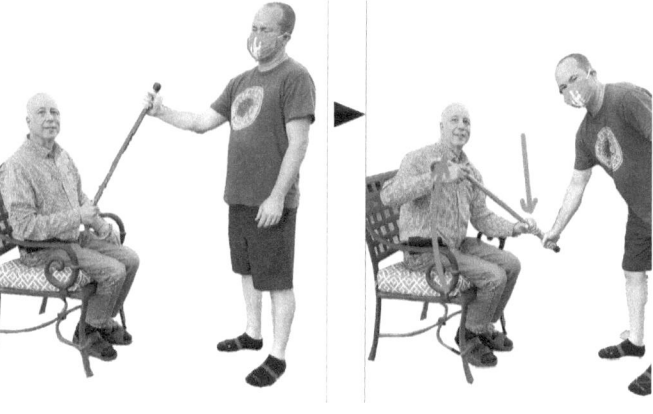

As you know, I'm not fond of strikes to the head, but this is one of the few exceptions. Re-read my warnings in chapter 7 about striking the head.

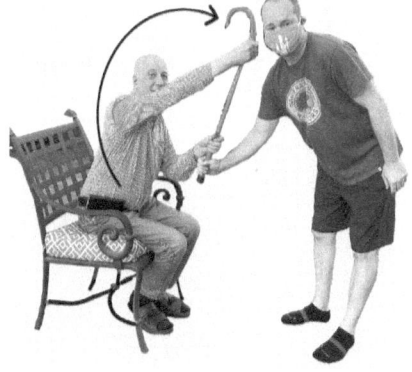

Chapter Thirteen

Cane Spinning

Cane Spinning Necessary

Cane spinning offers many advantages besides its stage-like glamour. Every cane user should adopt and perfect at least basic cane-spinning techniques.

Avoid Fights

In my opinion, a quick demonstration of cane spinning to an approaching evil-looking person will usually persuade that person that he does not want a fight with you. Do I have statistics to back up my statement? No. As far as I know, no studies have ever been done of the number of people who have been attacked while holding a cane, let alone if they did cane spinning before the attack.

However, one of the attorneys in our law firm did criminal work, and for fifteen years we had crooks sitting in our waiting room. Over the years, while they waited in our lobby, I talked to thirty to forty of them. They all said the same thing: they would avoid a target who appeared at all dangerous, challenging, or excessively time-consuming. To them it wasn't worth the risk.

Someone considering attacking a person with a cane is looking for an easy target. If they see you spinning the cane in a spectacular and potentially dangerous manner, they might decide not to run the risk of getting into a fight they can't win. You are showing clearly that you don't need the cane for support and that you have the know-how to maneuver it in a hazardous fashion. I believe cane spinning will cause well over half of potential assailants to pass you by and seek easier prey.

As you spin, yell repeatedly, "Go away!" or "Back off!" Surprisingly, police recommend also using profanity in your yell. They feel some criminals don't get the message unless it is coated with swear words. It's your choice. Most important, there is no downside to spinning the cane in front of a potential adversary.

Muscle Memory

Cane spinning teaches you how to handle the cane and perfect transitions. It also helps build muscle memory, so that you need not look at the cane to execute some of the moves. You react by feel and rote memory.

Look Ahead

One of the biggest mistakes is to look down and watch the cane's progress and location. Practice while looking straight ahead at the would-be attacker. The axiom is "As you practice, so shall you do in a real fight."

Side Body Spin

Direction of the Spin

The side-body spin can be done in only one direction. I know, because the first time I tried it, I hit myself in the head. You have to twirl counterclockwise. In other words, start at your feet and spin the cane toward your back. If you circle the other way, you are pulling the cane up toward your head, and you will probably get whacked.

Nature of the Spin

Start by holding the cane loosely in your dominant hand. Swing it backward and then over your head, and keep spinning. Note that I am looking forward and not moving my shoulder or elbow. The spinning is all coming from my wrist and hand. Don't move your shoulder; it should be stationary.

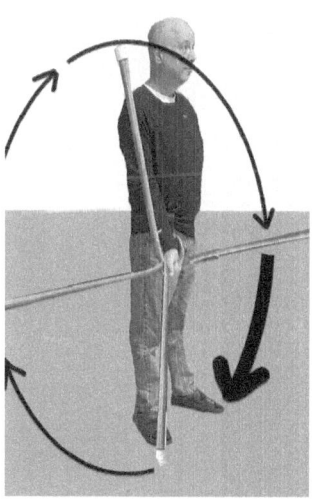
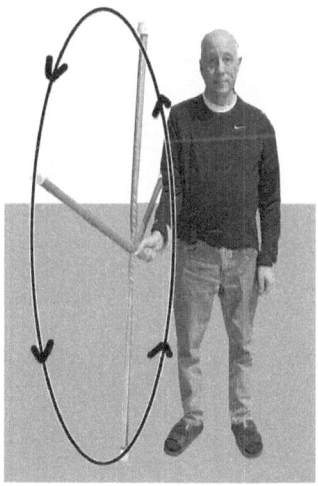

It doesn't take much effort to spin the cane in this

manner. Look at the two pictures on the previous page. They are the same image, except that the first was taken at a ninety-degree angle to my body and the second was taken face on as I twirled the cane.

Figure Eight Weave

The figure-8 weave, the most effective technique in this book and the most used by cane practitioners, was already discussed in detail in chapter 6. You should have it perfected.

Figure 8 Transfers

After you are competent and can make figure-8s fast and tight, work on switching hands. This is one of the simplest hand-offs in stick fighting. Just pass the stick from one hand to the other. It is an easy technique involving little skill.

Holster the Cane

Meaning of "Holster"

holster is to hold the cane by the crook, with the staff under that same hand's elbow, or if you have the cane tip face upward, then under the armpit.

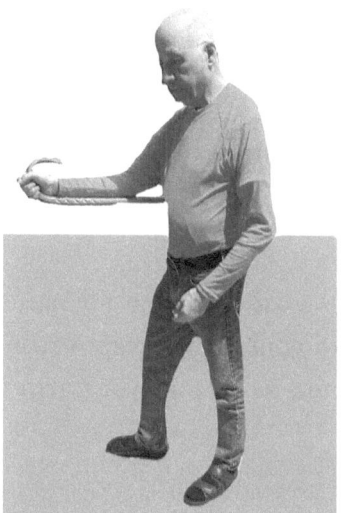

Locked if Crook is Face Down

When you holster the cane from a figure 8 or side spin, the stick will likely be in the crook-down position. If you try to strike and the crook is facing down, you can't swing the cane freely. The stick becomes locked by your elbow, and no strike is possible.

Reverse Cane Position

As I just mentioned, you cannot execute a horizontal strike from the holster position if the crook is facedown. So to make the cane ready for an attack, you must reverse the horn direction using a more mechanical switch that takes a while to master.

The cane goes around your wrist twice, but for part of the revolution, nothing is holding it to your wrist except centrifugal force. It will stay pressed to your hand as long as your arm is moving fast enough.

You might remember seeing demonstrations of centrifugal force by your high school science teacher. The teacher takes a plastic bucket with a handle and fills it with water. The instructor then swings the full bucket in swift vertical circles on one side of his or her body. The water stays in the bucket and doesn't spill, even when the bucket is upside down, thanks to centrifugal force. The water will spill only if the teacher goes too slow. The same principle applies when you are spinning the cane around your hand to change the horn's position.

Don't be discouraged if the cane repeatedly drops to the ground while you are mastering this technique. It takes time and much practice. Although this maneuver can be initiated from several different positions, the easiest way is to start with the tip of the cane straight up. The cane is held in my closed fist. Note that my thumb is sticking straight out. It becomes a guide for the cane during the spin. By the third picture, the hand is open, and at this point centrifugal force keeps the cane in hand.

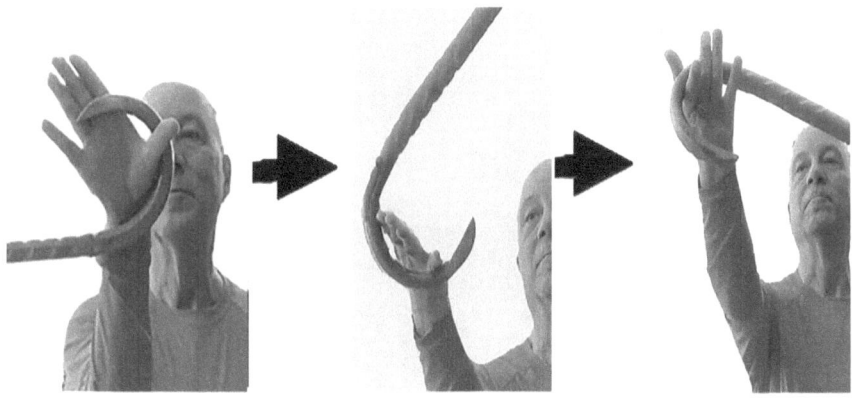

For the rest of this section of the revolution, the hand stays open. Physics keeps the cane next to the hand. To reiterate, if you do this twirl slowly, the stick will fall out.

By the time the cane is nearing the three-quarter point, the hand again closes around it. In this closed position, it draws the cane through the revolution.

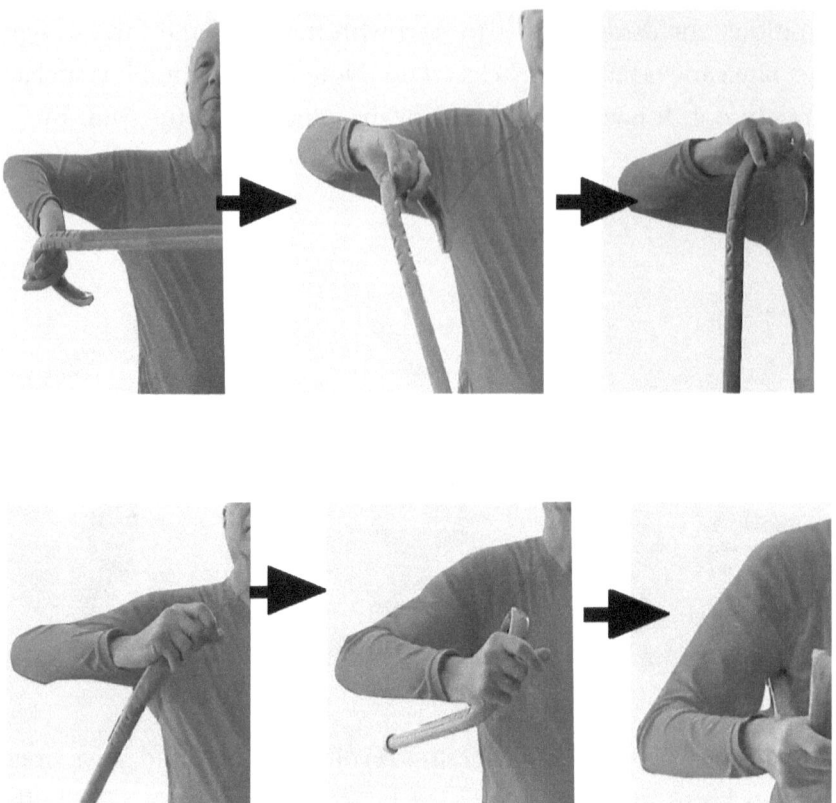

The final three pictures have to do with holstering the cane. Note that the cane, which would have been crook facedown upon completion, is now face up.

Horizontal Strike from the Holster Cane Position

OOnce the cane is holstered correctly, all you need to do is to twirl it horizontally in front and to the other side of you. It swings like a gate from the crook, which lies in your hand. This is a potent and quick strike and one of the main reasons you stand in the holster position. The shaft of the cane will swing below your holstered arm. Once you finish the first part of the horizontal strike to your other side, quickly and powerfully swing the cane back and holster it again.

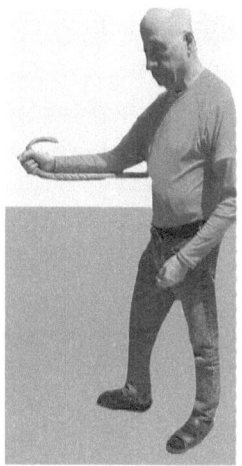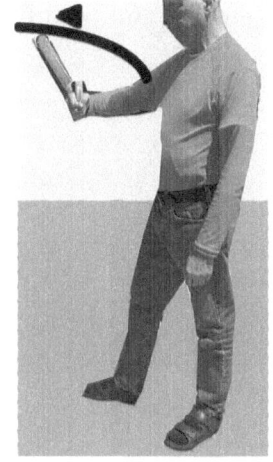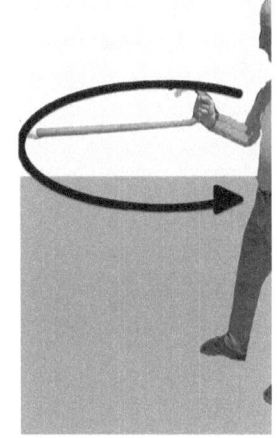

My Street-Fighting Kata

For Street Use

The cane-spinning form below is my idea of what is advisable to show someone approaching you that are to be taken seriously and not attacked. It covers the bare minimum and is not too long, which I find essential when on the street. You don't want to go on so long as to attract attention or seem like you are performing for yourself. This is why you do the reverse spin only once. When you do the form, remember to look straight ahead and not at your cane. The pattern is for use on the street.

Not for Kata Demonstration

Practitioners of judo, karate, cane-jitsu, and some

ju-jitsu systems use "kata" to practice their arts. A kata is a prearranged sequence of moves that is memorized, perfected, and choreographed for demonstrations. Each step is judged on its perfection, fluidity, body movement, and breathing. Many practitioners feel the kata is the core of gaining mastery over your techniques. The minimalistic form described below is far too short for use as a true demonstration kata but is excellent for the street.

My Demonstration to Potential Attacker

1. Two forward (side) spins on the right side of your body (right hand)

2. One figure 8 (right hand)

3. Switch hands and one figure 8 (left hand)

4. Two side spins on the left side of your body (left hand)

5. Reverse cane spin (left hand) if you are comfortble doing so.

6. One figure 8 (left hand) - with writst turned

7. Switch hands and one figure 8 (right hand)

8. Two forwards spins (right hand)

9. Reverse cane spin (left hand) if you are comfortble doing so.

10. Holster the cane (right hand)

How to Practice

First, work the form into muscle memory and practice it, so you are comfortable doing all the steps without thinking or looking. You should perform this "little kata" (demonstration) each and every time you pick up your cane.

Once you have perfected this, practice doing the form while walking. Walk forward and backward while doing the kata, so that multitasking does not slow you down. Finally, do the form with your eyes closed, so that you have the feel of the cane and, if you ever need it in a dark alley or dimly lit place, will have no problem working the form.

Why No Horizontal Strike

Once you have demonstrated the kata to a potential adversary, there is no need to elaborate on what you have already accomplished. Besides, why show a likely opponent your possible next move before the need arises? Finally, you should be doing a figure 8 spin to your potential opponent if he approaches after you have done my street kata.

Airplane Spins

An airplane spin looks like a helicopter rotor above your head. You raise your hand above your head and, while holding on to the crook of the cane, spin it around your head, usually for several revolutions.

Of all the cane spins you can do, this one generates the most speed and, therefore, power. Radar guns have clocked black belts reaching speeds of over two hundred miles per hour. I would use this spin only if I were sitting down (especially in a wheelchair) or facing multiple opponents. Other instructors may find other uses for this strike and employ it more frequently than I would.

Further Training

The two predominant cane self-defense systems in the U.S. are CaneMasters (the American Cane System) and American Cane Self Defense (ACSD). Both have practitioners across the U.S., and both offer classes over the Internet. Either one will suit you well and provide a solid base for self-defense techniques, quality sports training, and considerable exercise. For those interested in a comparison of the two systems, see the footnote beginning on the next page.

American Cane System

    The American Cane System (ACS), developed by Grandmaster Mark Shuey of Incline Village, Nevada, is a traditional martial arts–based system for the cane. Grandmaster Shuey is the founder of the modern martial arts cane movement in the U.S. and a twelve-time world champion in tournaments. The ACS progresses

Fn. 1 from previous page

through eight levels, teaching katas and one hundred essential self-defense techniques that must be learned in order to test for first-degree black belt.

The ACS system employs blocks, strikes, and jabs with the cane, as well as accompanying empty-handed techniques. Most ACS students have a martial arts background, and the cane is employed to support kicks and punches as an additional method of defending against an attack. However, the cane remains just one of the tools in the practitioner's arsenal, and not necessarily the primary tool. Most practitioners of the cane performing katas in karate and martial arts tournaments have been trained in the ACS system.S system.

American Cane Self Defense (ACSD)

American Cane Self Defense is a tactical cane system for self-defense developed by Grandmaster Joe Robaina of Miami, Florida. The system does not employ martial arts katas and is designed solely for tactical application in real-world self-defense situations. Previous training in martial arts is not required, and effective skills with the cane may be learned and employed by a beginning student of any age. ACSD is composed of three divisions: combat cane (spinning), self-defense, and fitness.

Combat cane spinning is the primary component of the ACSD system. As a tactical tool, it is used to simulate freestyle (non-scripted) defensive movements in varying combat scenarios. For training, it is used to teach a student to simulate tactical defensive combat while applying the techniques and movements learned in the ACSD program with speed, power, and accuracy. Combat cane spinning prepares the practitioner for defensive combat and refines footwork, timing, and coordination. In use, the practitioner executes a series of fluid defensive movements that simulate combat against one or more mobile opponents while executing strikes, parries, thrusts, and spins at varying tempos and heights. Combat cane spinning can be done solo or in pairs and shares some similarities with shadow boxing. While shadow boxing is usually stationary, combat cane spinning is mobile, as the practitioner is always engaging one or more moving targets. Tactically, combat cane spinning allows an instructor to gauge how their student would look (and perform) against one or more opponents at any stage of their training. When executed at the highest level, combat cane spinning becomes an art form and exhibits fluidity and elegance in the master's movements. A lengthy combat cane spinning session may constitute an entire workout.

Common Goal

When the cane is used for self-defense, the goals of both the ACS and ACSD are similar: they are designed to enable a practitioner to incapacitate an attacker

Fn. 1 continued

long enough to escape the area and make a report to law enforcement. In both systems the cane is always referred to as a "tool" or "personal protective device." The cane is never referred to as a "weapon," since it is designed only for use in mobility and self-defense.

Chapter Fourteen

Multiiple Attackers

In today's world, if you are attacked, it might be by two or more people. When the attack happens, they may attack as a coordinated group. Alternatively, it may be that the leader initiates the contact, and the others will join in moments later in support of their friend, and sadly because they might think it fun. Make no mistake, fighting multiple attackers is far more challenging and significantly more dangerous than fighting just one individual.

My roommate in college was walking down the street in broad daylight as two fellows approached him with smiles on their faces. Just before they reached my friend, they split in two and quickly attacked. Unfortunately for them, my friend was a black belt in karate and solid muscle. He kicked the first assailant between the legs so hard he picked them off the ground; the doctor had to do surgery to pull his testicles back down. The second mugger threw a punch which my roommate blocked, wrapped around his arm, and twisted his hips, breaking the arm badly.

The attack was in broad daylight, and only after the two gang members were on the ground rolling in pain, that the people watching on their porches finally phoned the police. It can be done, and you can defend against multiple attackers without being a black belt.

Pre-Attack Activities

However, Before the attack occurs, you should have considered "situational awareness," which includes the opportunity to run away before the encounter. It would be best if you also commenced proper breathing.

Situational Awareness

>Each situation is unique, and you must evaluate the circumstances as best you can. You should be more afraid in a seedy neighborhood at night while walking down a dark alley where two scruffy-looking individuals wearing shirts with hoods approach you. Sometimes, like my friend above, there is no warning.

>If you ever get the "sixth-sense" feeling that this local or potential situation might be dangerous, you should follow your hunch. Turn around and walk or run in the other direction. You can never get hurt from something you missed entirely.

>Assuming you haven't turned and disappeared, be aware of the situation. Where are the doorways, if any? Notice if there is a wall you can lean against, so nobody gets behind you if the condition turns ugly. Pick a direction you would run, if necessary. Is there gravel on the street or alley you pick up to throw at somebody? Can you take off your belt, so you will have a belt and a cane to use in self-defense? Are there potholes or debris on your path that you will want to avoid? Be hyper-aware of your situation and the condition of your surroundings.

Breathing

Remember from earlier chapters that deep, slow breathing relaxes the mind and calms you down. Such breathing will give your more energy. You will prevent hyperventilating and over-accumulation of carbon dioxide. Such inhalations will forestall going into a "flight-flight" response to the effects of norepinephrine (and later adrenaline). These hormones increase the heart rate, enlarge the eye's pupils, force extra blood to the muscles, change the body's metabolism, raise glucose levels, and gear for a fight or flight response from you.

Unfortunately, as it takes over your body, these hormones also restrict your thought process and logical reasoning, both of which you need in the fight. Finally, if you are fighting at least two guys, they will have more breathing power than one person. You need to control and regulate your breathing, so you don't run out of oxygen.

Select Target Areas

Try and decide beforehand if you reasonably feel this potential attack will be a life-threatening situation. Or, you need to be prepared during the actual attack if you feel your life is threatened. If you reasonably fear deadly force, you are justified in using deadly force in protecting yourself in most jurisdictions. (You should know the law in your state.) If you reasonably believe that great power is necessary, you would be within your rights to swing for the opponent's head and not just pressure points below the neck.

Use Your Cell Phone

If you have a cell phone, call for help. Also, try to photograph or videotape the attackers. Such action will help afterwards if you want to pursue legal action, and sometimes just the mere knowledge that they are identified might keep potential attackers from acting.

No Kata:

Earlier in this book, I suggested a short, quick pre-arranged demonstration of your mastery of cane fighting when facing a single attacker. Such a display often makes the potential assistant think you might be a "hard target," and not worth the risk and time involved to attack you.

With multiple attackers, the element of surprise is one of your most significant advantages. I would not recommend showing the "gang" your ability. You are already severely disadvantaged, and if they underestimate your power that helps level the playing field. Plus, they will think and act as though you do not have a weapon.

Defense Strategy for Two Attackers

Specific rules help in defending against multiple opponents. It would help if you relied on these rules, which have developed over thousands of years in martial arts. There are four cardinal rules: never get in the middle, move in a circular pattern, so you have a man between you and another assailant, keep moving and seeking the outside for an escape, and never fall to the ground.

Never Get in the Middle:

It is most difficult and impractical to fight two attackers simultaneously. You never want to stand still in the middle and let them both come for you. If they both arrive at the same time and are attacking from different sides, you are facing a near-impossible position. Look at the diagram below, on the top where you were in the middle. Each assailant is exactly four steps away from you and will probably strike you at the same time.

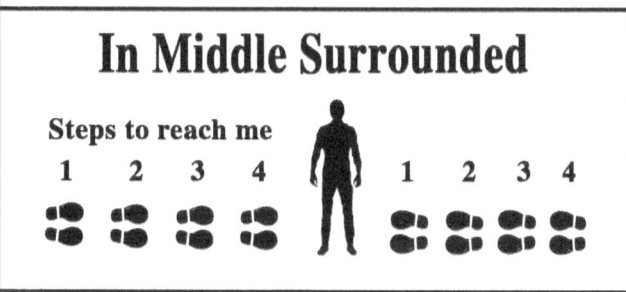

Compare your position to that at the picture below. If you suddenly and very quickly run towards one opponent, you can be one step away from him. You can then deal with just that one assailant because the other attacker is seven steps behind. The prime rule is that you only fight one person at a time.

Circle Around, So One Attacker is Lined Up Behind Another Assailant

In the above example, assume you have just disabled the first attacker, and the second foe is just seven steps behind and rushing towards you. Alternatively, rather than walking with the cane, you can parry his attack. You will then be on the outside of your attacker, and you can go around him.

In either case, grab this person's shit by the shoulder or back collar (depending on where you are standing). Use that person as a barricade. Twirl and drag him around so that he and your second attacker are in a straight line. If your disabled assailant has fallen to the ground, use him as a barrier. You stay on one side and keep the other attack on the other side of his fallen friend.

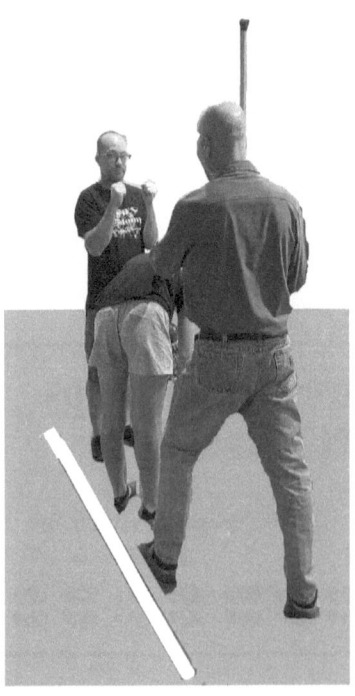

Same Shot, Different View

As long as you control the position of the injured mugger, you can keep moving in a circular pattern to keep the damaged person between you and the second attacker. So, if the second attacker moves three steps to his left, you will circle him three steps to your right, always keeping that attacker between you and your neutralized first attacker. The attacker can only reach you by striking over the top of his friend. But you have your cane with its extra long reach.

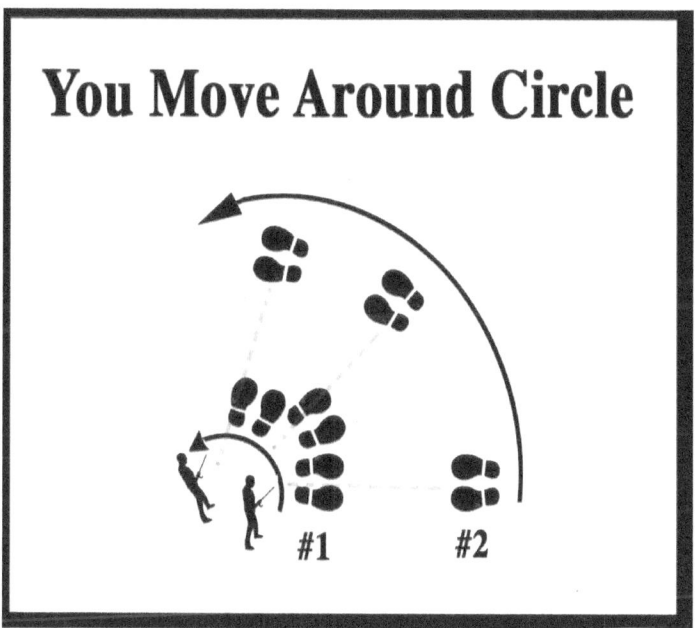

Don't Stop Moving

Never stand stationary. You keep moving in a circular pattern towards an outside opening. As soon as you find such an escape route, you should take it and run away. Your goal is not to win the fight and injure each attacker but to ultimately flee unharmed. This is not a game, and your safety is your top priority.

Never Fall to the Ground

Do everything you can to remain on your feet. If you ever fall to the ground, they can easily take your cane away from you and beat you with it. Most likely, they will also kick you in the head, Stomach, and or kidneys. On the ground, your number one goal is to protect your head by curl up in a fetal position and raising your hands around your face, elbows out.

You then hope to find a way to gain a standing position. Getting up from the ground is covered in books and Internet videos on unarmed combat. (It is also covered in chapters 32 and 33 in my book on unarmed combat, Escape Being Raped or Attacked.) Getting up is not easy, but it can be done successfully, especially with only two attackers.

Strike Hard

You may not always have the luxury or time for two strikes against an individual. You may need to keep moving to keep the two attackers in a line. So each strike must be powerful, and hopefully disabling.

Always Strike the Nearest Attacker

Even if you have not disabled your first attacker, if your second assailant approaches within striking or kicking distance, you must abandon the first individual. You need to meet and defend against the new attacker. You can't fight two active attacking individuals simultaneously.

You don't just ignore the first individual. You should

have grabbed his shirt, or otherwise gain enough control over him, that you can throw him between you and the second attacker. Even if the first attacker he's not disabled, he can still make an excellent barricade.

Defense Against Three or More Attackers

The same for cardinal rules or defense against two people apply to protecting yourself against several attackers. The main difference is that you want to keep moving towards the outside of the group. You never want to be in the middle. Keep finding a way to the outside. As soon as possible, run from the attackers.

The second significant difference with several attackers coming at you is that you may not have room to swing or cane. You might be forced to use it like a sword or a spear, and if you do so, don't forget that you have the backend of your cane (the crook) as well. Keep moving because you don't want someone to be able to grab your cane.

If the leader is within reach, he should be your first target. Often, if the leader and several of his friends are hurt, they will not bother to run after you when you escape.

Chapter Fifteen

Wheelchair Defense

Some of the self-defense techniques used by a standing person can be executed the same way while sitting in a wheelchair, while others need modification to be fully effective when delivered sitting down. For several reasons, fighting from a wheelchair is different from fighting in a standing position.

First, Newton's law applies. For every reaction, there is an equal but opposite reaction. If you strike without holding a wheel to prevent your chair from moving, it will roll in the opposite direction of your strike

Holding Wheel While Striking

Second, from a seated position you cannot use your legs and hips in your strikes, so your cane techniques will likely be slower and less effective than they would be for someone standing.

The third and most obvious difference is that you are half the height of most attackers. Surprisingly, that is as much a benefit as it is a burden.

Benefits

Few people know how to fight someone at waist height, so the attacker improvises by bending over, not realizing this puts him at a disadvantage. When a standing man bends down, his center of balance shifts from his hips (where he is most stable) to his sternum (solar plexus), where he is weak and off balance.

Being off-balance, your opponent can be easily thrown if you can grab him (and if you know some ju-jitsu). If he has already caught you, he is easier to throw with a ju-jitsu throw or drag-down.

By bending over, the assailant loses the ability to change positions quickly. He must first straighten up to move effectively.

Finally, statistically speaking, your opponent must limit and focus his attack on only half the area of someone standing.

If you have a cane in your hands, you are formidable with your extra reach. Always work with your strengths, and make your opponent play your game plan.

Canes have other benefits to wheelchair users. The tip can be used to drag an item on the floor to the chair where it can be easily retrieved. The crook end can reach things on shelves. The cane may prove useful even if you don't resort to self-defense.

Reduce the Target on Your Back

You also need to know that, sadly, many druggies and low-life criminals assume you are helpless and may try to strike or rob you. Your odds of being attacked are much higher than an ambulatory person. Cane-jitsu can help equalize the situation, but nothing, not this book or any weapon known to man, can totally eliminate the risk of an attack.

Don't Look Like a Victim

>When you roll down the street, do so with your head up high. Re-read the section in chapter 1 entitled "Don't Look Like a Victim." The same attributes that apply to an ambulatory person apply to someone in a wheelchair.

Self-Image in a Chair

>Wheelchair defense depends more on how you see yourself than on what techniques you know. If you see yourself as a lesser man, disabled, and pitied, probably no amount of self-defense knowledge will save you.

>The Mideast wars have, sadly, returned many veterans in wheelchairs, adding to the population of people already in chairs from illness and injury. There are many programs, including the Wounded Warriors Project and the Warrior Cane Project, and many individual self-defense studios that teach veterans how to defend themselves.

> As one wounded marine in a wheelchair said, "God help the man who attacks me. I'll chop him up in little pieces with my cane. A marine is always a marine, whether standing up or sitting in a wheelchair."

I admit that having disabilities makes it harder to see yourself as a complete man, and it can undoubtedly require more significant effort to protect yourself. But, it can be done if you accept what you can and cannot do.

You have to develop a fighting spirit, a belief in yourself, and an ability to take a risk. I know that for some wheelchair users, that is asking a great deal. I have found the best way to boost your self-confidence is to learn that you can compete with any man in a physical attack. That means you must have training in the cane until you feel confident.

If you are learning from a book, try taking one technique a week and practicing that self-defense technique until it becomes second nature. The weeks will pass quickly, and as your skills progress, future moves become easier.

Further Instructions

While I feel knowledge of the cane is sufficient for most ambulatory people, I recommend additional instruction for those in a wheelchair. There is too much risk you might be attacked when you can't get to your cane or where you might not be able to use it effectively. I recommend that all wheelchair users take either ju-jitsu or karate classes after mastering the cane. You need to know how to block punches and other attacks with just your bare hands. Karate teaches you to block and strike. Ju-jitsu shows you wrist locks, and armlocks are taught in ju-jitsu and aikido. Because you are such a target, and attacks can come from any angle, I believe you need more diversity of defenses than just the cane. Your decision will probably depend upon time commitment, transportation, finances, and instructor quality. What follows is my opinion; I'm sure each instructor has his own.

Karate

Karate teaches all types of effective blocks to different attacks. The techniques are sound, practical, and for most peoples who use wheelchairs, easy to use. However, karate punches involve pivoting the entire body when throwing a punch, which is what makes them so devastating. In a wheelchair, where you can't use your hip or legs, a karate punch will be significantly less powerful. It will probably not stop an attack unless you hit a pressure point. Kicks are usually beyond the physical ability of most people sitting in a wheelchair.

Ju-Jitsu

In searching for a ju-jitsu school, you need to find one that teaches wrist throws and arm locks. Some ju-jitsu systems teach only cage fighting (tournament fighting in an octagonal ring), which will probably not meet your needs.

Mixed martial arts ("MMA"), dominated by Brazilian

ju-jitsu taught by the Gracie System, is currently the most popular style taught in the U.S. Even they admit that tournament work is quite different from street struggles

Selecting a Teacher

When selecting a doctor, you should never choose one you sincerely dislike. The same goes for martial arts teachers. Also, make sure your instructor has taught others in a wheelchair. I would ask the instructor for at least three names and phone numbers of current or former students who use wheelchairs. Call them. Teaching individuals in wheelchairs is sub-specialization that requires far more knowledge than just cane, karate, or ju-jitsu techniques.

Stop with Back to Wall

IIf you decide to stop on the sidewalk, try to do so with a wall at your back. In that position, nobody can attack you from behind. Everyone will see somebody defenseless an individual in a wheelchair, not realizing the strategic position you are in or that you are ready to defend yourself.

Other Weapons

Taser

Even though this is a book about using a cane as a self-defense weapon, I would advise carrying a taser if your state allows it. Again, this is only my opinion, but I feel a taser is a far more powerful weapon than a cane. Tasers work from as far away as fifteen to twenty feet, depending on the model. They penetrate clothing to cause a disabling shock. However, if you can't carry a taser, I feel a cane is a second-best weapon.

The states are split on the carrying and use of a taser. I am in Arizona, which does not even regulate tasers and allows you to get one without a permit. (Ariz. Rev. Stat. § 13-3117(E)(2)). Many other states have similar laws. Check your state law, or call the local police station. They are usually accommodating.

Pepper Stray

I am not overly fond of pepper spray and tear gas for two reasons. First, in a strong wind, some of the mist can blow back to you, and if you aim poorly and miss the head, it may not disable an assailant. Second, in some cases such weapons have a severe residual effect on people who have been sprayed. For those who favor such non-lethal weapons, use them with caution.

If you are going to use pepper spray, don't carry it on your keychain or in your pocket. Carry it in your hand, visible for all to see. The time it takes to pull the canister out of a pocket and take the top off can be crucial in an emergency. Further, a potential mugger generally looks at your hands.

If he sees mace, the mugger usually figures you could be a "hard" (difficult) target or one who can arouse bystanders, making it more difficult for the mugger to disappear. Often, he will ignore you in favor of easier-looking prey.

Wheelchair as Weapon

The use of your wheelchair as a weapon is discussed later in this chapter.

Summary

Regardless, since you are at a disadvantage in a wheelchair, you need your primary system to protect yourself. If you don't want a gun, knife, or taser, then I feel the cane is your best device. And after you master the cane, I encourage you to take additional classes in ju-jitsu or karate.

Terminology and Advice

According to the World Health Organization definitions[1], people in a wheelchair are considered "handicapped," in that they must use a wheelchair to get around.

Some of the self-defense techniques while stilting in a wheelchair are

---

Fn. 1. The most commonly cited definitions are those defined by the World Health Organization, in The International Classification of Impairments, Disabilities, and Handicaps.

Impairment. An impairment is any loss or abnormality of psychological, physiological or anatomical structure or function. More traditionally, an impairment is usually a difficulty with a structure or organ of the body. Such impairment can be due by a correctable condition (such as poor eyesight), or by an uncorrectable disorder (such as polio).

Disability. Disability is any restriction or lack (resulting from an impairment) of ability to perform an activity in the manner or within the range considered normal for a human being.

Handicap. A handicap is a disadvantage for a given individual that limits or prevents the fulfillment of a role that is normal.

the same as for a standing person. However, other procedures need modification to be fully effective when delivered sitting down.

Individualized Approaches Needed

> Per the WHO definition, depending on the person's impairment, the sitting self-defense techniques might need tailoring to that individual's abilities. A person with multiple sclerosis might require different methods from an individual with cerebral palsy. Somebody with paralysis of the legs can use their upper body differently from people with other impairments.

Who Am I to Talk

> I sometimes hear from people in a wheelchair, "You don't understand what it is like." And you are right, I don't fully comprehend the restrictions, frustrations, and occasional depression from being in a chair. But I do have some insight. My wife once broke both her legs and ankles in a head-on car accident. For a year, she lived with two full-length casts and used a wheelchair. More important, I understand the limitations of a disability. I started mastering the cane at age seventy-three, after recovering from a heart transplant.
>
> The limitations that come from having had a heart transplant are severe. The reason a person with paraplegia can't walk again is that science cannot yet connect nerves. When they took out my old heart, they had to sever all the nerves to free the organ. My new heart has no nerves connected to it. If I go from lying down to standing up, my heart does not receive a signal to pump more blood. If I want to practice cane techniques, I can make only one or two moves, and

then I have to stop and rest. My heart thinks I'm still sitting down. It won't increase my heart rate to meet my needs.

When I teach, I don't tell my students about my limitations, and I talk in detail about the techniques while recuperating between demonstrations. I doubt the students even realize I'm limited. This is a long way of saying I have some comprehension of the limitations you face daily. Your limitations may make it harder to protect yourself, but I have found that people who use wheelchairs are among the most determined and dedicated learners.

Escape from Cane Grips

Frequency of Cane Grips

One of the most frequent complaints of wheelchair users who study the use of the cane is the frequency with which the attacker manages to grab the cane shaft. Assailant grips should cause no significant concern if you have practiced grip release until it became second nature. Because grip release is not as glamorous or exciting as strikes and twirls, I suspect cane grip releases are given too little emphasis.

Escape Using Cane

Reread the section in chapter 15 on cane grip escapes. I urge you to master grip releases before you turn to cane strikes and blocks.

Escape from Wrist Grip

While this is supposed to be a chapter about using the cane to defend yourself, it would be unrealistic to expect you to hold cane at all times. First, you are not always anticipating an attack and may have your cane in a holder on the back or side of your wheelchair. Second, most paraplegics require both hands to maneuver and power the wheelchair.

I was shhowing one wheelchair user how to protect himself with a cane, and he said "but the attacker grabbed my wisrt and my cane is in the back of my chair." That was when I realized you needed to know an unarmed wrist escape in can you ever find yourself in that situation.

Assume someone is going to grab you, which is one of the most common attacks countered on the street. You need to know how to handle the situation, so that you can release yourself from his grip and have time to grab your cane. I am going to discuss only one unarmed wrist release, but there are numerous unarmed techniques available for every other kind of hold.

Front Flex Throw
Unarmed Defense

Assume the attacker grabs your outside wrist with his hand, so his knuckles are pointing outside your body. He grabs your left arm with his right hand. There are four steps to your defense technique.

Hitchhike. Hitchhike. Make a fist. Now, from your elbow, rotate your arm in a circular motion so your fist is now pointing skyward, almost like you are hitchhiking. Your shoulder does not move. If your opponent sees shoulder action, he may have time to react. This technique's effectiveness is the circular movement pivoting from the elbow, which prevents his pectoral muscles from coming into play.

Pry Free. There should be a slight separation already visible between your wrist and the heel of his hand. Place your right thumb on the back of his knuckles, and pry your left wrist from his grasp by working against the thumb. Then grab his right hand, so both of your thumbs are against the backs of his knuckles.

Ninety-Degree Bend. Now fully bend his wrist at ninety degrees to his arm. Picture a brick wall from the floor to the ceiling running right through his hand, and move his flexed wrist up and down that invisible wall. Do not go forward or backward, just up and down on a vertical plane.

Break His Balance. Push your attacker down, destroying his balance. Now, if you want to move him in any direction, flex so his knees are bent, for as long as he is not straight, he cannot turn around and hit you or move. It is also an ideal position for a throw.

Optional Fifth Step: Throw. To throw the attacker, should you so desire, twist his wrist sharply to the left as you swing the rear of your chair to the right. Keep rotating, and he is forced to throw himself to the ground or break his wrist.

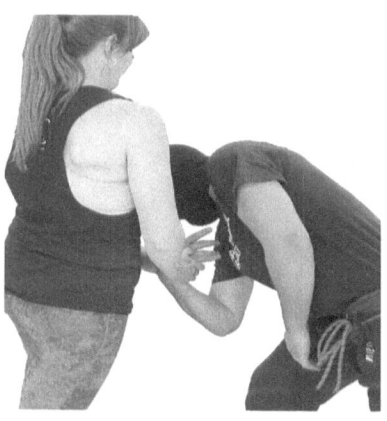

Practice with the Other Arm. After you have practiced and perfected this technique, practice it with him grabbing your other hand, until you are equally comfortable on either side. After all, you can never be sure which wrist an attacker will grab. After a short while, it shouldn't matter which arm he grabs.

Hidden Purpose. I presented this throw not only for your use but also so you will have some idea of ju-jitsu joint throws. If you do decide to pursue training in ju-jitsu, ask the instructor to show you three or four ways to escape from a wrist grab. He can show in on another (in order words, he need not each the arts to you). If he can't show you moves like the one above, go to a different ju-jitsu school.

> I went to a highly rated ju-jitsu school for a short time, before realizing the school's philosophy was fighting in the ring for sport. Their goal was to take the opponent to the ground and beat him on the mat. I believe that in a street fight, the last thing you want to do is be on the ground. So be sure to ask questions of your instructor.

When Approached

On the street, you survive by using whatever works for you. One benefit of learning multiple moves or positions is that you can select the one that best fits your build, style, and risk approach to fighting. Perfect the techniques you most like first, and after you have worked those techniques into muscle memory, go back and work the others. Also, don't be afraid to experiment.

Ready Position

> When an individual approaches and is within, say, fifteen feet, you should be in your ready position. The benefit of the ready position is that you are prepared for your next move, yet you don't look threatening. The most common wheelchair ready position is just to rest the cane tip on the floor between your feet.

On Guard Position

> I recommend a ready position with the cane face up, prepared to strike or block if your attacker comes within five feet of you. Your non-dominant hand should be in a fist facing the sky, about shoulder high. This hand is ready to hit, shake off a grab, or block a punch.

Note fist ready to strike or grab

One- or Two-Handed Strikes

Ted's Rules

I have to preface my rules with the caveat that other instructors may vary in their opinion. Use what best meets your needs.

Rule #1. Use two-handed jabs, if possible, over one-handed cane swings. One-handed strikes are slower and less powerful in a wheelchair, since your hips and legs cannot provide additional power. Therefore, you run a higher risk of the opponent grabbing your cane.

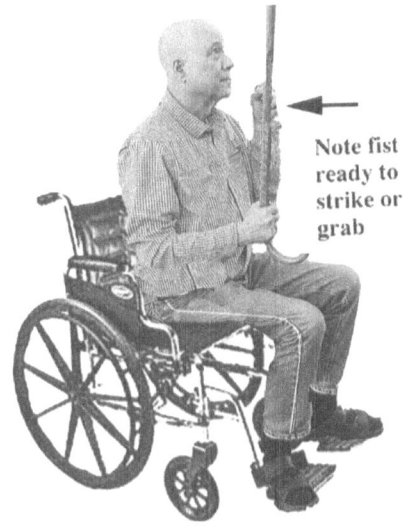

Rule #2. The deciding factor will be whether you (a) have the brakes on, (b) are holding one wheel of your chair, or (c) have no brakes on and no hands on the wheels. With both brakes on, while you can't move your chair freely, the chair remains stationary, and you can jab or swing without worrying about the chair moving.

With one hand holding a wheel, you have only one hand free to keep the cane. This situation mandates one-handed jabs and swings

If you have no hands on the chair and the brakes are unlocked, the chair might rebound in the opposite direction for several inches, if you jab forward and strike your attacker. The wheelchair might not move with a one-handed swing.

Rule #3. Some people have practiced enough hitting rubber tires or other objects to know how to handle their wheelchair and still deliver a jab or swing with one or two hands, and even control their chair. Those individuals should use any technique with which they are comfortable.

Unarmed Block

Unlike someone who is standing, I believe anyone in a wheelchair should know to block a punch unarmed. This allows you to block and strike simultaneously and to block if you do not have your cane handy. Blocking is not hard because, in your lowered position, punches will almost always be thrown at your head.

Using the Simple Block

This block covers the whole side of your face. Just make a fist and put it next to your ear, as if you were scratching your ear. The punch will hit your hand, lose all its momentum and power, and land harmlessly and painlessly. It is a simple block because you do not have to track the blow and seek to deflect it. Instead, you let the strike come to you and catch it somewhere on your forearm. Many students have initially said it sounds too simple to work, yet it works well and effectively against roundhouse punches. This block is often used in the ring during professional boxing matches.

Variations of the Block

If your attacker is punching toward your midsection or parts of your body besides your head, move your forearm to protect the body part he is targeting. It takes more coordination for lower blocks, since you are reaching out to the punch, which is unlike waiting for the blow to come to you.

Some people do the same action but use their hands to push to punch aside. If I am not using a classic karate block, I use the side of my hand to strike the person's wrist (like a judo chop). It is all the same action, just a slightly different part of the body. However, the palm push and the judo chop take more skill and practice than the simple forearm block. Select the block that is most comfortable for you and perfect it.

Combination Block and Strike

If my history is any indication, some will find a combination block and punch challenging. If you do, the answer is simple: don't use such a technique. Others, if they practice it long enough, will find the combination block and strike a useful method of defense.

Twirl Show-off

In a wheelchair, you face the same decision as an ambulatory person when someone approaches you and you feel that he may be dangerous. He may or may not actually pose a threat, but you want to discourage him from considering an attack. If so, you can do the cane-spinning kata from chapter 13. It will work from a chair, although it has less power and speed when sitting. Usually, the brakes are off on your wheelchair when twirling.

Wheelchair Protection

Recognize that some of the techniques described in this book cannot be employed in a wheelchair. Most can be adapted, but not all. Usually the striking, blocking, and self-defense techniques work for people in wheelchairs. There are also some special skills involved in striking from a wheelchair. I do not feel the cane alone is sufficient to defend anyone in a wheelchair, and your safety is paramount, so this chapter includes some unarmed techniques.

Strike or Jab

If your wheels are unlocked and you are striking or jabbing with one hand, you will probably want to keep your other hand on the wheel. If you are right-handed, you will probably keep your left hand on your left wheel. At the same time, you might lean to the left, to give more support to your right hand. With your right hand, jab the stick forward into the attacker's groin, or swing at his legs.

Instructors may vary in their advice, but I prefer that people sitting limit strikes to below the belt. Those pressure points are very open, and attackers are unused to protecting their lower bodies. Also, when the attacker is leaning forward, it is  harder to reach the solar plexus and other above-the-waist pressure points. I specifically exclude the head as a potential target (with a few exceptions) because of the possibility of brain damage and the risk of the attacker grabbing your cane.

Of course, if both brakes are on, you can make one- or two-handed strikes. The problem with having your brakes on is that you lose your ability to maneuver the chair to match your opponent's movements.

Pop Strike

One-Handed Pop. If someone is annoying you and is very close to you, (about a foot away), but does not appear dangerous, you can do a pop strike. It causes some pain but does typically no real damage. It is useful because it is so quick.

All you do is whip your wrist while holding the cane. Have the horn facing up and towards you (if you mistakenly strike with the horn facing the opponent, the wood will turn on impact). Whip your wrist forward, and the crook will hit the person in the solar plexus. Immediately return the stick to its original position.

Double Pop. You can do the same strike, with more force, if you use two hands. For a two-handed pop strike, be sure to keep your top hand behind the cane. If your knuckles wrap around the cane, they risk getting hit when you strike the opponent.

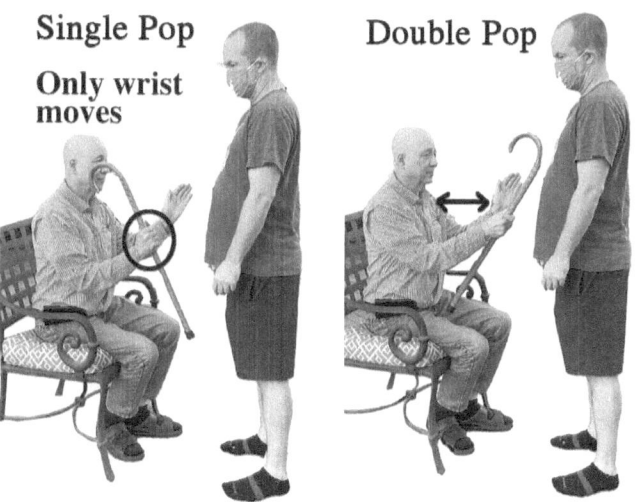

Wheelchair as a Weapon

Your wheelchair is a surprisingly effective tool because it hits so low and is so unexpected. You can drive your footrests into an attacker's shin with surprising power. It's painful, and often the assailant will bend at the waist and lean forward. That is an ideal position for a powerful punch to the head.

I know one wheelchair user who very effectively kept his chair almost perpendicular to the attacker. When the opponent got close enough, he swung the chair in a circular motion, driving the side of his footrest into the assailant's leg bones. You can also run over your assailant's feet with the small wheels on the front. Then, when he is unable to move, you can strike with your cane and drop him to the ground.

If someone comes up behind you, most wheelchairs' rear handles are on a level with his groin. If you can, back into him, aiming a handle between his legs.

You can lift the side rail out of its fitting and swing it like a club. You can use it to block punches or strike with the hard edge of the round pipe.

I even read about one wounded marine veteran who was thrown from his chair to the ground and thrashed the assailant with the detached wheel of his chair. I'm not saying the wheelchair is a great weapon, but don't discount its value in a fight.

Neck Twist Takedown

This technique is a very effective one, but it also has to be used with great skill, so that you do not break the attacker's neck. You are low to the ground, and the attacker must lean forward toward you. If he grabs your lapels, starts to choke you, or otherwise grabs you so that both your hands remain free, you can use the neck-twist takedown. Put your left hand on the back of his head, and grip his chin with your right. Then twist his neck, slowly forcing him to let go. It is a violent twist.

You can turn the attacker in a circle and drop him to the ground. This move is especially effective and used by many wheelchair users. I want to reiterate my earlier warning that this can be a dangerous move and cause a broken neck. But with practice, it can be done safely and effectively.

Attacked from Behind

Grabbed from Behind

Sometimes an opponent will come up behind your chair and wrap his arms around you in a rear bear hug. At first, this attack seems terrifying until you realize how easy it is to break. Since this is a book on cane defense, if you have your stick handy, whack it behind you three or four times until the person gives up and retreats. If you cane is not available, it is easy to throw the instigator over your shoulder.

Chair Pushed from Behind

What do you do if someone maliciously pushes your wheelchair from behind, refuses to talk to you, and moves the chair at a rapid pace? Your responses depend so much on your confidence and the facts of your situation. There is no magic bullet for this solution.

Put on Brakes. If you can, quickly put on the brakes

to slow down and stop. If you slam on your brakes, be sure to hold on so you won't be thrown suddenly off the chair as it loses its momentum. If you can stop, follow up by striking the pusher using the rear of your elbow into his body. However, if you fear that at that speed, your hand might become caught in the spokes, skip this step. It is not worth risking severe additional injuries.

Quick Pivot. I've not seen this move in action, but it was described to me by a wheelchair instructor for veterans. Reach down and take a strong, firm hold of the inner wheel on one side, and try to stop it from spinning. At the same time, push forward on the other wheel as hard as you can. The combination will cause the chair to turn 180 to 360 degrees almost instantaneously. A good chair will pivot stably without overturning. However, I would undoubtedly practice this move many times before using it in the street.

Insert into Spokes. If you can't put the brakes on or do the above pivot, try putting a pen or other available object (even a cane, if available) into the spokes to slow down the wheelchair. Some suggest jumping off when the chair is slow enough, but that might be as risky as staying in the chair. You would have to decide on the spot which is your best option.

When Stopped, Whack him. Once the chair slows down, the pusher is usually hunched over at the waist, with his face near yours. Turn to your side, even if you can only turn a quarter-turn. Whack him several times with the point of your elbow, or swing the elbow in a blow against his jawline. Don't try to hit your assailant on the chin, as that is the strongest bone in his face, and you can severely injure your hand or elbow striking that location. Alternatively, try hitting him with the back of your fist (called "uraken" in karate, if you want to Google the term).

Use a Cane. If you have a cane, swing it behind you, hitting any place you can find on his body. Repeat the swings until the opponent lets go of your chair and retreats from the scene.

Conclusion

I know life is not always fair, and there are no "free rides" in the universe, but with the information in this book (and extra training, if you choose to avail yourself of it), you should be comfortable wheeling yourself down any street and feel relatively safe.

Chapter Sixteen

Elderly Senior Defense

The mere fact that you are elderly and have limited energy should not limit your ability to use and learn self-defense techniques with the cane. It only means you can't exceed your physical and medical limits and must use techniques within your ability. More importantly and sadly, you are often deemed an easy target on the street.

You Can Learn

I know you can handle a cane, because I can do it, and I am almost seventy-five and have had a heart transplant. People with paraplegia remain immobile because science cannot reconnect nerves. When they removed my old heart, they had to cut all the nerves connected to it.

My new heart is not connected to any part of my nervous system. Normally, when you get up from lying in bed, your brain knows you are now standing and need more blood flow. But with no nerves, my heart assumes I am still lying down. It senses no reason to increase the heart rate, so I must be careful getting up. Because of this, I sometimes act age eighty-five or ninety and can hardly move. Yet I can still teach cane defense, sometimes only one move at a time, and other times several techniques before I am exhausted. If I can do the cane, so can you!

Your first step should be a talk with your doctor to make sure he approves of your learning cane defense. There are moves you can do sitting down if you find it hard to stand. If you need a cane when standing, you can hold your normal cane with one hand and use the other hand to swing a second cane. If your balance is shaky, you can lean against a wall and swing a cane (which works for certain defenses but not for all).

Like many elderly cane practitioners, you may find that the use of the cane and its exercises improves your balance and increases your strength. In a way, cane defense is as much a sport as fencing, boxing, or wrestling. The key to learning any sport when you are older is not to look at where you want to be. Instead, evaluate your performance by how far you have come from when you started. Only when you are entirely comfortable with the sport should you look at what you ultimately hope to achieve.

For seniors I encourage group lessons, because it is easier to practice with others and more fun. When I teach a class for seniors, I have six rules:

1. Do what you are capable of doing. Don't let the instructor "bully" you into exceeding what your body is capable of. If you feel dizzy or short of breath, sit down and watch for a while. If a joint hurts when you move it, don't move that painful joint during the technique, and if it bothers you at rest, sit down and watch, or do a modified version of the movement.

2. If you can't make a move, don't worry. But do some movement. Do what you are able to do, even if it's just the merest part of the technique. Any training is better than no action. Besides, what you can't do today, you might achieve later on.

3. If you are having trouble, ask for help. When I help a student, I talk loud enough so others can hear. Often, other students will benefit from your correction, just as you benefit from theirs.

4. Always warm up before you practice.

5. I always announce near the end of an individual exercise or training technique when it will end. You do better and might try harder if you know there are only four more repetitions (then three, two, and one). I also announce how long the rest period will be and ask if everyone is ready before going to the next cane procedure.

6. If you can't hear me, raise your hand and wave, or shout louder. Don't stay silent if you can't hear. The noise in the room ("ambient noise"), hearing aids, or just older inner ear parts can make instructions harder to hear and understand.

Warm-ups

Before you start, make sure the instructor has you warm up your muscles. All professional athletes, even in their prime, warm up before performing. When you are older, you have less muscle, and your muscles are looser and less resilient than they once were. Warm-ups help you reduce the risk of injuries. For more information on why you need warm-ups, reread chapter 1.

In my class, I use the National Institute on Aging's Go4Life Exercises (currently at https://www.youtube.com/playlist?list=PLmk21K-JuZUM4HTrJ7hrJ8yxhToKkJT8a8). They include five easy exercises recommended for older adults and take almost five minutes. (Of course, other instructors may have different routines.)

1. **Marching in Place**. Slowly, then speeding up slightly, march in place. Move your arms forward and back as you "walk."

2. **Sideways Step**. Step to the left with your left foot. Bring your right alongside. Then step back with your right foot, and finally place your left foot beside your right foot. Move your arms up and down while moving your feet.

3. **Arm Stretches**. Put your arms halfway up, meaning your upper arm and elbow are level with your shoulders, then raise your hands to the sky, then return to shoulder height.

4. **Sitting to Standing.** Sit in a chair, then stand up using only your legs. Sit back down. Keep your arms forward at shoulder height throughout.

5. **Ankle Stretches from Chair**. Sit in a chair and put your legs out straight, about shoulder width apart. Point your toes down toward the ground and then upward (rolling your ankle).

Don't Look Like a Victim

Many people are selected as a target for criminal activity because they look easily intimidated and an easy mark. Reread the part of chapter 1 entitled "Don't Look Like a Victim." It won't stop all attacks at your age, but it should reduce your likelihood of being attacked.

Also, practice "situational awareness." Before stepping out of a store, your house, or any building, develop the habit of looking left, right, and straight ahead for anyone who might be troublesome. If you see such a person, ask someone to walk you to your car, or wait inside the store until that person leaves. Be aware of your environment.

For example, in my book Escape Being Raped or Attacked, I discuss a wide variety of situations and tell readers what to notice and how to react. For walking alone on the street, I urge:

> If it is a route you will often be taking, make the acquaintance of the people and business owners along the way. Smile and greet them every time you pass. They can become a safety net for you and will look out for you as you walk past them.
>
> If possible, wear shoes you can move in. Take off your high heels and carry them in your purse as you put on flat surface shoes. It would help if you were free to move quickly in an emergency, and it is tough to run in the wrong shoes.
>
> Walk in the middle of the sidewalk, not right next to the building where people could theoretically reach out from doorways and grab you. At corners, do not cut the angle short but walk wide so you can see around the corner before you make the full turn. Ignore strangers and do not talk to people who ask you questions or make comments as you walk down the street, head held high. Smiling in an open and friendly way and talking to anyone invites strangers to get close to you. Such is the opposite of what you are trying to accomplish.
>
> If you are walking down a long road with few people and businesses, walk facing traffic so you can see

approaching cars. Otherwise, you cannot see anyone approaching you from behind in a car.

Learn the Techniques

Introduction

    A. **Speed and Duration.** Each class and each person is different, so I never set a certain amount of time for a particular technique. I am more concerned with teaching a move until the class understands and is comfortable with it, before I teach another movement. One of the benefits of working with older adults is that they tend to be willing to master one technique before they are overwhelmed with more.

    B. **Why Start with Double Pop.** Whatever move you learn first, it should be effective and simple and require little energy. The first move makes you feel that you can master the cane and that it will work for you. The double pop, followed by the single pop, accomplishes these purposes.

    C. **Not Repeat Other Chapters**. You can use many of the techniques that appear elsewhere in this book. However, rather than repeating that material, I will simply refer you to those pages. Realize that while most seniors can do pops and jabs, depending on your balance and strength, you may not feel comfortable with swings.

Pops and Jabs

    A. **Single and Double Pop.** Refer to chapter 15 ("Wheelchair Defense"), pages 192 and 193. The first technique to learn is the double pop, a two-handed move, performed while sitting down. Next is the double pop while standing up. Then practice the single pop while seated before proceeding to the single pop standing up. The last technique is to use the pop while striking a throw pillow or anything moderately solid.

B. **Straight Jab**. The details and pictures are in chapter 8 ("Strikes") on page 92 to 94. Aim for the front of the neck, solar plexus, and groin.

   1. **Learn the Individual Moves**. Do one jab to the neck, then step back to your original position. Repeat until you start to become comfortable with the technique. Next, do the jab to the middle of the chest until you are somewhat confident of the strike. Last, perform the groin jab. The individual locations help you build muscle-memory awareness and realize three different easy targets.

   2. **Learn Jabs from a Chair**. After you have mastered and are satisfied with your ability to strike from a standing position, learn the same moves while sitting in a chair. You never know what position you will be in when attacked, plus the repetition reinforces the standing jab.

   3. **Learn While Stepping Sideways**. Slide left sideways as you step and jab to the left. Keep sliding and striking left until you are near the wall, then slide sideways and jab to the right. Keep poking and sliding to the right until you reach the other side of the room.

4. **Learn While Stepping Forward and Backward.** Step forward with your left foot as you jab straight forward. Keep stepping and striking until you near the front of the room. Now hit as you step back. Keep poking and sliding to the rear until you reach the back of the room.

C. **Resting Position to Swing to Groin.** Here you have the cane tip point touching the ground. You swing it quickly upward to waist height (if your condition permits) without moving your elbow. It is a quick and effective strike between the legs, which generally leaves the assailant crouched on his knees or lying on the ground. See chapter 7 ("Pressure Points"), page 85. After you are comfortable with this swing, practice doing it against a moderately firm pillow.

Swings

A. **Nature of a Swing.** Swinging a cane is more analogous to swinging a whip than a baseball bat. In any event, you swing the club by the horn (U-handle), since at your age, you would likely find it too difficult to swing the rod with the heavy, weighted U-handle at the far end. The ankles, lower leg, and knee are the safest targets; the neck and head are potentially dangerous, harmful targets. (Review chapter 7, "Pressure Points," for more information.) To swing a cane, you must have enough balance, and some may not have that ability. However, standing against a wall may allow you to swing the cane. Since jabs and pops can be sufficient, you can still defend yourself even if you can't swing a cane.

B. **Groin Strike.** Begin with the cane tip on the ground. Pivoting from the elbow, swing it upward into the groin. (See chapter 7, page 85, "The Testicles.") All of the below are the same movement.

   1. From Front Clothing Grab.
   2. From Front Wrist Grab.
   3. From Two Arms on Shoulders.
   4. From Front Finger Pointing.

C. **Low Diagonal Strikes.** These are the regular diagonal strikes from waist or shoulder level, directed to the knees, leg, and ankles. (See chapter 3, page 35 and chapter 9, page 104, except no block involved).

D. **High Diagonal Strikes.** These strikes, which start with the cane held shoulder high with the tip higher, are very effective but should be done only by those who can sustain their balance. (See chapter 9, page 105, except no block involved). After performing the strike stepping forward, do the same stepping backward and striking until you reach the front of the room.

E. **Combination Swings.** Finally, practice doing two swings in a row, so that in case the first swing doesn't work, you are automatically starting on your second strike. It is burned into "muscle memory." You may not need the second strike, but it is beneficial to be ready.

Swing at Target (Bob)

When I first started teaching ju-jitsu self-defense to women, many ladies seemed to have difficulty practicing striking a man in the groin.

I told them if you can't do the strike in practice, how do you ever intend to perform it on the street when you need it? I would do the strike, showing them that it was not sexual or indecent but practical and efficient. It helps if you are realistic.

I found that practicing without actually striking a target makes it hard for seniors to believe the techniques will work. Hitting a target gives seniors pride and a feeling that the cane strikes and jabs will work.

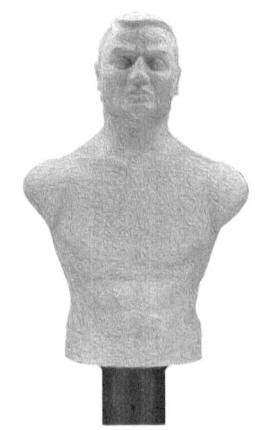

I used "Bob," a rubberized man made to take the strikes of feet, punches, and canes. I think it cost about $300 new on Amazon, and a used one would probably be half that on eBay. Of course, you can buy simple punching bags and striking cushions for $30 to $40 and up. Even less expensive but still effective would be an old sofa cushion.

Defense Against Specific Attacks

The last part of my advanced seniors' class involves responding to various assaults, such as a wrist hold, cane grips, bear hugs, and other attacks. Much depends on your ability, needs, and endurance. Go through this book and pick out moves you would be able to practice.

Exercise Resistance Bands

Use rubber or latex "exercise resistance bands" with rubber loops at each end to get in shape. Generally, they are color-coded as to the resistance levels; you need one that requires only a light amount of strength. Loop the cord's ends over the ends of the cane, and put the middle on the floor. Now sit down and put your feet on the band. Push the wooden shaft upward and in other directions. It is a great way to strengthen your muscles. A good exercise therapist or the internet can teach you many ways to use exercise bands.

Make This Author's Day

If this book was a help to you and you are a member of Amazon.com, please write a two or three-sentence book review.

It will help others select a book on this topic, and it will certainly make my day.

In Amazon, type in this book title. Then about two-thirds of the way down on the left, just below "customer reviews," you will find a button that says [Write a Customer Review].

Please. And thank-you!
Ted H. Gordon

Appendix

Where to Buy Self-Defense Canes

Where to Purchase Canes

Below are some of the combat canes you can buy from Cane Masters and American Cane Self Defense, the two leading cane systems in the U.S. I am not associated with either organization; the information below is from their websites. The prices below are those posted for the base models and may change over time, and the wording is theirs (not mine).

You can also find canes on the Internet, some even from other countries. Mainly, you want a cane that is an inch thick and preferably solid oak, hickory, or other hardwood. Also, the size of the crook (curved handle) must be wide enough for your use, preferably the width of a neck.

Dislike of Drugstore Canes

You can use an ordinary cane as long as it is strong enough to withstand horizontal compression— meaning when you swing it at someone somewhat like a baseball bat, the staff won't crack. Unfortunately, too many $15 drugstore canes are poorly made for such use and might break. I recommend purchasing a true self defense cane.

My First Cane

My first cane was from CaneMasters, the "Double Grip Walking Cane," which I purchased with no extra options or accessories. It cost, as of this writing, is $75. Certainly, as I progressed, a few years later, I purchased other canes. But the basic cane was more than enough to provide what I needed.

The options can be confusing, and one friend, likened to buying a car because they had so many extras and he didn't know if he needed any of them. The "options" add beauty to the cane, help it age better, but (in my opinion) do not add much additional protection for a beginner.

Cane Masters Canes
https://www.canemasters.com

Cane Masters Tactical Training Cane: The Premium Select Grade oak training cane is crafted with a full set of upper grips and "inside cut" to the horn. The cane has been soaked in mineral oil and proprietary polymers for 48 hours before finishing with two coats of hi-gloss tung oil. Base cost $75 with polymers and tung oil.

Viking Master Cane: The Viking Master Tactical Cane is designed for members of the military, law enforcement, and special operations. It is crafted from 1-1/8" Thunder Oak Stock, soaked in a blend of mineral oil and polymers, has grips carved the full length of the sides of the shaft as well as on the crook and comes with your choice of Palm Rest Design as well as stain and 12 coats of hand rubbed tung oil finish. It is one of our strongest and most beautiful canes. $355

"Don't Tread on Me" Cane: This special anniversary cane was produced for the Fourth of July, 2020 by Cane Masters to celebrate the nation's founding. It is produced in hickory with a masterfully carved eagle horn and distinctive "Rooster tail" palm rest. The color is a special "oxblood red" and is finished with 12 coats of hand rubbed tung oil. Each cane is serial numbered engraved with the famous "Don't Tread on Me" coiled snake. $400.

Tactical Mini-Master Glass Breaker. The new 24 inch long Mini-Master Glass Breaker Cane is crafted from Hickory and designed to be carried inside your automobile for emergencies, such as glass breaking to escape a flooded or burning automobile. If you live near rivers, canals, lake, or ocean, having a means to break out of a submerged car is recommended by authorities. The new Mini Master features a palm rest and steel striking stud, and well as a rounded metal tip for breaking side windows. The 24 inch length is also ideal for maneuvering inside a vehicle and ideal for personal protection. The base cost is $120.

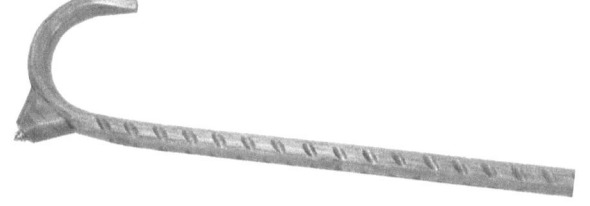

Medical Alert Card. Cane Masters customizes each card to the customer's individual needs. Cards are produced using the same equipment states utilize to produce driver's licenses. Each card is heat in full color on rigid white plastic. The colors are vibrant and will not fade. Cost $25.

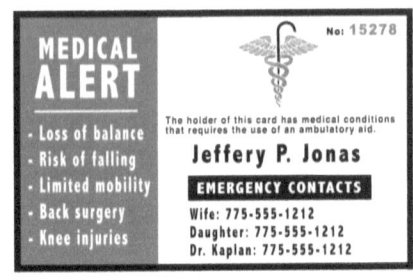

American Cane Self Defense Canes
https://www.americancanesslfdefense.com

American Cane Self Defense Canes did not respond to my free request to include pictures of their merchandise so you will need to look at their website if you want more information.

Index

The author during his
third-degree black belt test

Index

== A ==

Adams's Apple, 82-83
Adrenalin, (See fight-flight response)
Aggressor, not recognize cane as dangerous, 1
Aikido principles, 137-138
Airplane spin, 159-160
American Cane Self-Defense System, 161
American Cane System, 161
Armed robber, my philosophy, 90-91
Armpit, 84
Arms, 87
Attack probability, in wheelchair
  Increased, 175
  Reduce probability, 175-176
Attackers, Multiple
  Pre-Attack, 164-166
  Three or more, 171
  Two attackers, 166-170
Avoiding fights by cane spinning, 149-150

== B ==

Backpack to keep hands free, 17
Back stance, 58
Bear hug
  From back, 125-127
  From front, 127-129
Bob striking figure, 44
Blocks
  Blocks vs. parries, 47-49
  Inside, 48, 189-190
  Nature of, 48
  Outside, 48
  Wheelchair, unarmed blocks, 188-190

Blocks with cane
  Block and step back, 99-100
  Block only forearm, 94-95
  Boxer's left jab, 106-108
  Defense (See "defense to punches")
  Procedure, 50-55, 99-108
  Pushing block, 51-52
  Right and left punch, 105-106
  Swing block, 51-52
Bob rubber target, 44, 207-208
Boxer's left jab defense, 106-108
Breastbone, 84
Breathing
  Breathing technique, 98
  Countering adrenalin rush, 96-98
  Effect on fighting ability, 97-98
  Fight-flight reaction, 88-89

== C ==

Cane
  Aggressor fail to recognize cane as dangerous, 1
  Buying a defense cane, 4, Appendix A
  Cane wallet card, 5-6
  Cock the cane, 42
  Danger of using, 6-8
  History as self-defense device, 1
  Learning as a senior, 191-201
  Making a cane, 10
  Mobility impaired users, 2-3
  Parts of (crook, horn, shaft, tip), 11, 42-43
  Recovery, if taken, 41-42
  Regular canes limited, 3 (fn. 1), 4
  Size, correct length, 12

Unarmed attack against, 41-42
Cane Grips, defense against
    Advice, 137-141
    Standing, 141-146
    Wheelchair, 146-147, 182
Cane Spinning,
    Airplane spin, 159-160
    American Cane Self-Defense
        System, 161
    American Cane System, 161
    Avoiding fights by, 149-150
    Figure-eight cane weave, 152
    Holster the cane, 62, 152-154
    Reverse cane position, 154-156
    Side body spin, 151-152
    Street fighting kata, 157-159
Choke from back
    Cane defense, 131-132
    Nature, 129
    Unarmed escape, 129-130
Choked from front
    Cane defense, 124
    Nature, 121-122
    Unarmed escape, 122-123
Cock the cane, 42
Cocking fist before punch, 91-92
Crock of cane, 11, 43

= = D = =

Danger of using cane, 5, 7-8
Defense to holds
    Front bear hug, 127-129
    Front choke, 123-124
    Lapel grips, 132-133
    Rear bear hug, 125-126
    Rear hand choke, 129-132
    Wrist grips, 133-135, 182-183
Defense to Kicks, 113-120
Defense to punches, using the cane
    Block and step back, 99-100
    Boxer's left jab, 106-108
    Leg-throw, 108-110
    Pre-emptive strike, law, 95
    Right and left blow, 105-106
    Right blow, blocked, 99-108
Disclaimer, Waiver, and Release,
    viii - ix
Double pop, 192-193, 204-205
Don't look like victim, 12-16, 175-176,
    202-203

= = E = =

Elderly can defense (See senior's
    defense)
Escapes (Defenses)
    Front bear hug, 127-129
    Front choke, 123-124
    Kicks, 113-120
    Lapel grips, 132-133
    Punches, 99-104
    Rear bear hug, 125-126
    Rear hand choke, 129-132
    Wrist grips, 133-135, 182-183
Exercise resistance bands, 208-209
Eyes, 81

= = F = =

Fight-flight reaction
    Breathing technique, 98
    Countering adrenalin rush, 96-97,
        96
    Effect on fighting ability, 97-98
    Fight-flight reaction, 88-97,
Fight, goal of, 16
Figure-eight cane weave,
    Effectiveness, 70-71
    Importance, 67-68
    Performing the technique, 72-73
    Spinning, two types, 68-69
    Use in the street, 74
Fritz handle cane difficult use in self-
    defense, 4
Front bear hug
    Cane, 128-129
    Nature, 128
    Unarmed defense, 128-129
Front choke
    Cane defense, 124
    Nature, 121-122
    Unarmed escape, 122-123
Front-flex throw, 183-185

= = G = =

Goal of a Fight, 16
Grayson Study, 13-15
Grips
    Cane grips, 137-147

Lapel grips, 132-133
Wrist grip escape, 133-135, 182-183
Groin, 85-86

== H ==

Handicapped
    Definition, 180 (fn. 1)
    See "wheelchair"
Hands free, necessary, 17
Head, 78-80
    Danger, 78-79
    Eyes, 81
    Injuries, 78-79
    Temple, 78
Holds (See defense to holds)
Holstering the cane, 62, 152-153
Hook, 11, 42-43
Horn as part of cane, 11
How to Practice, x – xi, 43-46

== J ==

Jabs
    Body supports strike, 30-31
    Definition, 29-30
    Pressure points, 33
    Shoulder, doesn't move, 30-31
    Standing perpendicular, 32
    Seniors using, 205-206
    Two motions, 30
Ju-jitsu training, 177

== K ==

Karate
    Bob striking figure, 44
    Karate vs street fighter kick, 115-116
    Karate training, 177
    Makiwara board, 43
Kicks
    Defense to, 117-120
    Karate vs street fighter, 116
    Not frequent, 113-114
Knees, 86

== L ==

Lapel grip escapes
    Cane defense, 133
    Nature, 132
Law regarding canes
    California Penal Code §22210, 7
    General law allows, 5
    Must claim medical not weapon, 6
    Pre-emptive strike, law, 95
    Self-defense basics, 95
    Wallet card to carry cane, 5-6
Law regarding weapons
    Cane legal only if claim medical, 6
    Shillelagh, 5
Leg-throw defense, 108-110
Legs, 87

== M ==

Making a cane, 10
Makiwara board, 43
Medical Device, cane as
    Code of Federal Regulations, 3
    Wikipedia defines, 3
Mobility impaired users,
    General use, 2-3
    Lean against building, 2
    Sit on bench, 2
    Sit on sidewalk, 2
    Wheelchair users, 2, chapter 15
Multiple Attackers
    Pre-Attack, 164-166
    Three or more, 171
    Two attackers, 166-170
Muscle memory, 95-96

== N ==

Neck-twist takedown, 194-195
Neck, side of, 81-82
Need for self-defense, 18-19
Newton's first law in wheelchair, 173
Newton's first law in wheelchair, 165

== O ==

Offset cane difficult use in self-defense, 4

On guard stance
    Jabbing, 61
    Other hand, 63
    Swinging, 60
    Wheelchair, 186

= = P = =

Parries
    Parries vs. blocks, 48-49
    Procedure, 49
Pepper spray, 179
Police
    How explain cane, 6-8
Pop strikes, 192-193
Practice
    how to, x-xi, 43-46
    Muscle memory, 95-96
Pre-emptive strike, law, 95
Pressure points (front of body)
    Adams's Apple, 82-83
    Armpit, 84
    Arms, 87
    Breastbone, 84
    Effects, 33, 77-78
    Groin, 85-86
    Head, 78-80
        Danger, 78-79
        Eyes, 81
        Injuries, 78-79
        Temple, 78
    Knees, 86
    Legs, 87
    Side of neck, 81-82
    Sternum, 84
Punches thrown at you
    Armed robber, my philosophy, 90-91
    Block and step back, 99-100
    Block only forearm, 94-95
    Boxer's left jab, defense, 106-108
    Breathing (fight-flight reaction), 96-97
    Cocking fist first, 91-92
    Law self-defense basics, 95
    Leg-throw, defense, 108-110
    On guard stance, 60
    Right and left blow, defense, 105-106
    Right blow, blocked, 99-108
    Right-handed, mostly, 89-92
    Roundhouse vs straight punch, 92-94
Pushing block, 50

= = R = =

Ready position
    Standing, 60
    Wheelchair, 186
Rear bear hug
    Cane defense, 126-127
    Nature, 125
    Unarmed defense, 125-126
Rear hand choke
    Cane defense, 131-132
    Nature, 129
    Unarmed escape, 129-130
Reduce attack probability, 175-176
Reverse cane position, 154-156
Right and left blow, defense, 105-106
Right blow, blocked, defense, 99-108
Right-handed punches, mostly, 89-90
Robber armed, my philosophy, 90-91
Roundhouse vs straight punch, 92-94

= = S = =

Self defense
    Danger zones with canes, 40
    Wristwatch, danger looking at, 55
Self-defense canes
    Need for self-defense, 18-19
    Shillelagh
        Benefit, 4
        Legality, 5
    Special self-defense cane
        Nature, 4
        Legal if medical and not weapon, 5
        Purchase, 4
    Cane wallet card, 5-6
Self-image in wheelchair, 175-176
Senior's Defense
    Bob rubber target, 74, 208
    Don't look like victim, 12-16, 202-203
    Double pop, 204-205
    Exercise resistance bands, 208
    Jabs, 205-206

Swings, 206-207
Walking a frequent route, 203
Warmups, 203-204
You not too old to learn, 199
Shaft as part of cane, 11
Side body spin, 159-152
Situational awareness
    Consequence of ignoring, 21-23
    Improve awareness, 26-27
    Nature of, 23-25
    Sixth sense, 25-26
Size, correct length, 12
Speed of cane swing, 37-39
Stance
    Back stance, 58
    Flexibility allowed, 59
    Holstering the cane, 62
    Natural stance, 57
    On guard stance, 61
    Partially disabled stance, 59
    Ready stance, 60, 61
Sternum, 84
Straight punch vs roundhouse, 92-94
Street fighting kata, 157-159
Strikes with cane
    Definition, 29
    Jab, 29-30, 32
    Pop strikes, 192-193
    Strikes in wheelchair, 173, 187-188
    Swing, 33-35
    Two strike combination, 35
Swing
    Bob rubber practice device, 44, 207-208
    Diagonal, 43-36
    Makiwara board, 43
    Not like baseball swing, 34
    Power and speed, 38-39
    Procedure, 33-34
    Speed of swing, 37-38
    Seniors using, 206-207
    Tires as striking device, 45
    Two hundred mph swing, 39
    Types of strikes, 34-35
Swing block, 51-52

= = T = =

T-handle cane difficult use in self-defense, 4
Taser, 178

Temple, 78
Tip as part of cane, 11
Tire, device for cane practicing, 45
Twirl, wheelchair protection, 191
Two hundred mph swing, 39

= = U-V = =

Umbrella for self-defense, 10-11
Visualization, 96
Victim, don't look like
    Grayson Study, 13-15
    Introduction, 12-13
    Seniors, 12-16, 202-203
    Wheelchair users, 175-176,

= = W = =

Walking a customary route, 203
Wallet card to carry cane, 5-6
Warm ups, 16, 201-203
Weapons
    Law allows to carry
        General law, 5
        Wallet card to carry cane, 5-6
    Shillelagh, 4-5
    Special self-defense cane
        Nature, 4
        Purchase, 4
    Umbrella for self-defense, 12
    Wallet card to carry cane, 5-6
Walking a customary route, 203
Wallet card to carry cane, 5-6
Warm ups, 16, 201-203
Weapons
    Law allows to carry
        General law, 5
        Wallet card to carry cane, 5-6
    Shillelagh, 4-5
    Special self-defense cane
        Nature, 4
        Purchase, 4
    Umbrella for self-defense, 12
    Wallet card to carry cane, 5-6
Wheelchair
    Advantages in a chair, 174
    Back to wall, 178
    Block to a punch, 189-190
    Cane grab escapes, 137-142, 144-145, 182

Defense problems, 173-182
Don't look like a victim, 175
Handicap definition, 180 (fn. 1)
Ju-jitsu and Karate training, 177
Neck-twist takedown, 194-195
Newton's first law, 173
On-guard and ready positions, 186
One- and two-handed strikes, 187-188
Pop strikes, 192-193
Self-image when in chair, 175-176
Strikes and jabs, 191-192
Twirl for protection, 191
Weapons (pepper spray and taser), 178-179
Wheelchair as weapon, 180
Wheelchair pushed from behind, defense, 196-197
Wheelchair throw when attacked from behind, 195-196
Wrist grip escapes, 133-135, 182-183
Wristwatch, danger looking at, 55

www.ingramcontent.com/pod-product-compliance
Lightning Source LLC
Chambersburg PA
CBHW030905080526
44589CB00010B/149